oasis TRYING TO FIND A WAY OUT OF NOWHERE

JILL FURMANOVSKY
NOEL GALLAGHER

oasis

TRYING TO FIND A WAY OUT OF NOWHERE

1994 – 2009 / 2025

T&H

ROLL WITH IT
VERSE G HOLD
C-B-A
C-B-A x2
CHORUS F-G x3
F-C-D-C-B-D
VERSE G HOLD
C-B-A
G
C-B-A x2
C-B-D
G
2 ROLL WITH
CHORUS F-G
VERSE G HOLD
C-B-A
G
OUTRO → C-B-A
end on G
INTRO
VERSE
CIGS & ALCOHOL
INTRO 4 CYCLES GUITAR
E E
VERSE E E F# A
E E
VERSE E E F# A
E E
BRIDGE A E A E
A E D A
CHORUS EF#GDA EF#GDA
SUPERSONIC
F# A B
2 ROUND ARE WAY
3RD VERSE GFC GFC GFC GFC
GFC GFC GFC GCGF
3RD CHORUS DG DG DG DG
DCBA#AG
MID8 COME IN ON 2ND CYCLE
CCCCG CCCC
CCCCG
OUTRO GFC x10
THEN RUN ON C
REPEAT
ROUND ARE WAY
VERSE
BRIDGE
CHORUS
OUTRO
ROCK & ROLL STAR
INTRO GUITAR
B.E.B.E.C#A.B.E.
ROCK & ROLL STAR
VERSE B.E.B.E.C#A.B.E.
B.E.B.E.C#A.B.E.
BRIDGE G#E B G#E B
G#E B A F#
A E B
A E B
A E B
A E
VERSE B.E.B.E.
3 ROCK & ROLL STAR
CHORUS A E B
A E B
A E B
OUTRO A A A A
F#E F#E F#E F#E
F#E F#E F#E F#E
F#E F#E F#E F#E
F#E F#E F#E F#E
E → D → A

CIGS & ALCOHOL
4 CYCLES GUITAR THEN
DON'T LOOK BACK IN ANGE
INTRO
BRIDGE
CHORUS
LIVE FOREVER
LIVE FOREVER
CHORUS
VERSE
CHORUS

CONTENTS

NOEL GALLAGHER

We loved Jill from the moment she rolled up at the Corn Exchange in 1994. I met her on a stairwell backstage. She kind of reminded me of a dinner lady – and that's not an insult. It's a compliment because my mother was a dinner lady! Then, during the gig, I'm kinda fucking rocking out and there in the pit is the dinner lady with a professional camera. At the time she was working on a book of her photography called *The Moment* and I saw an early draft of it. The first photo in it was a picture of Paul McCartney outside his house taken by Jill as a schoolgirl. She was looking to end the book with a contemporary band that was on its way up. We were just blowing up at that point, so we were perfect. After that initial shoot she appeared at everything we did.

To us, and again this is not an insult at all, she looked like all our mums. She's kind of the same size as my mum. With our band we always had women working round us. One of the really clever things that our management did was understand that if a bunch of guys worked with us it would all be over. We were very respectful towards Jill. She's one of those rare people involved in the arts who's got virtually no ego. We were young lads in a band, full of drugs, in the nineties. Some crazy shit went on. But I never saw her get offended by any of it.

Jill's a quiet person, working in a very loud world. She disappears into the crowd or stands in the shadows at the side of the stage or follows you around the dressing room, and you forget she's there. I'm really comfortable around her and I just completely trust her. She's the best, do you know what I mean...? When I look at Jill's photographs, I always think to myself, I wonder where that fucking jacket is...? Where is that jacket?! Because she always got me in really fucking striking clothes and then I'd spend a year looking for them.... Over time the friendship becomes more important than the work and then the work gets better. Now it's like she's part of the family. Another thing I admire about her is her work ethic. I've never, ever, ever seen her without a camera. Ever. Maybe she takes it to bed with her!

She's photographed everyone, and in every possible scenario – Bob Dylan, Pink Floyd, the Sex Pistols, Blondie, Amy Winehouse and many, many more. And her portrait of Charlie Watts, which won an award in 1992, is incredible – one of my favourite photographs of all time. I'd seen it in a magazine before we met but didn't realize it was by her until several years later.

Jill's work is so varied: there's stuff that has made it onto album covers, live shots, candid shots, polaroids – everything. I don't think you could pigeonhole her as a photographer. That candid shot of us at Schiphol airport is one of my favourites. We're absolutely rat-arsed and Bonehead puts himself on the baggage conveyor belt – her photo captures the spontaneity and sheer joy of the moment perfectly.

Her photo of our first ever stadium gig at Maine Road, Manchester, in 1996 is a fucking great picture. It's significant to me because I stood on those terraces as a child, and I still support the club. But it also sums up that period. And it tells the story of the connection between the band and the audience. That picture says to me that everybody in that stadium is with us heart and soul. There's something else. It's instinct and a kind of magic – that's what it is, it's magic.

When you get into music you're generally too young to attend concerts but you're not too young to look at photographs, so your first point of contact with rock stars is the picture, or the artwork, which generally is a picture. You could argue that the picture is equally as important as the music. Whenever I bought a new album, I would stare at the record sleeve for hours waiting for it to speak to me in some way, waiting to find some meaning in it. All the great photographs are silent, but they speak to you, right? Jill's photographs have that quality; they just say something to you. I guess they're shot with love for the art itself, and with respect for the artist, and all that comes through in the photos.

I hate photoshoots. I can't stand them. I much prefer a photographer to follow me around for eighteen hours, snapping away. I'd rather do that than stand for eight minutes posing. I don't think I've ever had a discussion with a photographer telling them what I want. I'd rather let them do their thing and bring something out in me that I hadn't known was there. I don't know whether Jill edits her photographs of me sympathetically before showing them to me, but I haven't ever seen a bad one. I see something in those photographs that is real to me. Most of the time Jill worked with us it's been kind of snapping away in dressing rooms and stuff. And that, to me, is real.

She is a very, very dear friend of mine and it's been a honour to have been associated with her for thirty years.

INTRODUCTION

JILL FURMANOVSKY

It began with a concert at Cambridge Corn Exchange in December 1994. I had just found a publisher for my book *The Moment: 25 Years of Rock Photography*. It took the form of a diary, beginning with me as a Beatles fan in 1965 and featuring my work as a chronicler of the music scene during the seventies, eighties and early nineties. I was looking for a band that was up and coming – a band that had potential for greatness – to end the book, but one that would also mark the beginning of something new.

Music journalist Daniela Soave usually had her finger on the pulse of new talent in music. A year earlier, in December 1993, she had insisted that I go to see Jeff Buckley at a small club in London. That was a seminal moment in my life. So, when she recommended that I check out Oasis and put me in touch with Johnny Hopkins – their insightful press guy at Creation Records – I didn't hesitate to accept his invitation to see the band in Cambridge, and the greatest chapter in my working life as a photographer began.

I had a feeling the gig was going to be something special before I even laid eyes on the band. It was the queue of excited people, many of them super cool teenage girls, snaking down Wheeler Street and right around the block. It looked like a picture I'd once seen of Beatles fans queueing for the Cavern Club in Liverpool.

I was introduced to Noel Gallagher briefly before the gig began: he was friendly and low key. But in the photographer's pit the magic revealed itself. Here was a band that shone from the inside out. Their power was subtle because physically not a lot happened on stage.

The singer, Liam, was superb, but he just stood at the microphone with his hands behind his back and snarled into it, or he stared over the heads of the crowd like a menacing statue. He had charisma all right, but it was tightly packed into his posture rather than embodied in his movements. When he wasn't singing, he sat motionless on the drum riser. Noel was an inspired guitarist but there was no jumping around and no grimacing solos. As for Bonehead on rhythm guitar, Guigs on bass and Tony on drums, they hardly moved, looking to Noel for direction.

The effect of the performance on the audience was certainly not negligible. The atmosphere in the room was almost hysterical with excitement and the songs powerful and profoundly moving. Intrigued, I did my thing.

After the show I re-met Noel and Bonehead briefly, noted that my old friend Chrissie Hynde was backstage talking to Mark E. Smith of The Fall and that Patsy Kensit was looking lustfully across the room at Liam Gallagher, who was a lot more animated off the stage than on it. The A listers were checking out the new blood.

The band liked my pictures, which is what I hoped for because I wanted to take more. Christmas 1994 came and went and in January, at the invitation of Johnny Hopkins, I began to document the band's activities, beginning with the video shoot for 'Live Forever' in Portland Place, London. That led to a PR shoot in San Francisco later that month when they were on a brief tour of the West Coast. I continued by joining them – including a spell on the tour bus – during their US tour in March 1995. That is when I began to fall in love with the characters. Bonehead was the glue between the brothers and defused tensions with his gift for making everyone laugh. He just has one of those faces and doesn't mind being the butt of jokes. He was often teased for being a Manchester United fan – the only one in a sea of pale blue City fans. Guigs had a serenity that drew me in – he was relaxing to be with. Tony looked great in photos and had an edgy presence. That tour was the last time I photographed him with the band. He was replaced in April 1995 by Alan White.

I worked with Oasis intensively from 1995 to 1997 at the height of their popularity. I was experienced in the rock business, and they were just beginning. It was natural that I should feel protective of them. All the media attention and the phenomenal speed of their rise to super stardom was extremely stressful. It was hard to take it all in.

Liam could be difficult: he tested me out at the beginning. Photographer's small talk was not tolerated. He was and still is a 'wild card', unpredictable and reckless, but that is what makes him a 'proper' rock star. He could also be sensitive and kind. What helped with our relationship was the realization that we share the same birthday – 21 September – nineteen years apart but soul twins.

Noel is gifted not only as a songwriter and guitarist. Journalists love to interview him because he is witty, honest and insightful. He also has a tremendous work ethic. He carried a heavy burden within Oasis, keeping everything together musically, as well as doing most of the press interviews. In addition, he worked closely with me and others on choosing images for press use and record covers.

Noel and Liam Gallagher gave the band its unique DNA and they were a gift to any photographer. In my case they allowed closeness and almost unlimited access, just as Elvis had done in the early fifties with the great photographer Al Wertheimer, one of my heroes.

What they didn't have the patience or incentive for was spending a day in a photography studio changing clothes and posing in different set-ups. They were known to walk out of shoots that were meant to last a day after only fifteen minutes, particularly in the US. Being a quick worker was probably the chief asset I had as a photographer as far as they were concerned.

I try to be a low-key presence when shooting on tour or in a recording studio with musicians. In their case I would go to the soundchecks, hang out in the dressing rooms, photograph the concerts and join them on the road and in recording studios.

After each show the fun would begin for the band and road crew. There were many long drinking sessions in hotel bars and wild nights reported over breakfast by bleary-eyed musicians nursing hangovers. I usually went to bed early with a cup of tea. Once they got used to my presence, they no longer noticed me – I was like a member of the road crew – and I was able to continue documenting their working lives until the band split up in the summer of 2009.

I was forty-one when I began working with Oasis, just ten years younger than the Gallaghers' beloved mum, Peggy. I was somewhere between a much older sister and a maternal figure. It was a great place to be. I had photographed Pink Floyd, Bob Marley, Led Zeppelin, The Who and many other great artists of the rock 'n' roll era.

In particular, I was a contemporary of the punks: all of us winging it, none of us trained professionally, all determined to make our mark in a fleeting moment of creative energy.

↓

22 DECEMBER 1995
CREATION PARTY
LONDON, UK

Noel and Jill outside the Halcyon hotel, London, in front of the Rolls Royce given to Noel as a Christmas present by Creation Records.

Oasis seemed to blend all the eras I'd lived through, from the genius of the Beatles to the best of the seventies rock bands, combining them with a healthy dose of punk's arrogant irreverence. Oasis were the last great rock band of my career, and, as this book was going to press at the end of May, I had a brief and inspiring glimpse into their next phase – the 2025 reunion. Bring it on!

The work shown here represents only a fraction of the photos I took of the band. When they eventually imploded in 2009 the only surprise was that they had managed to stay together for so long. The comings and goings of various members had always changed the band's character, but it was the chemistry between Noel and Liam Gallagher that was, and is, its rocket fuel.

Oasis, like all the great bands I have worked with, have a rare kind of chemistry that has no formula and cannot be manufactured. In a way, such music doesn't even belong to the artists. Its power and potency belong to all of us who hear a pulse of ourselves in their music.

Where were you while we were getting high? We were right there with you and your gift will live in us forever.

DEFINITELY

RELEASED	29 AUGUST 1994
RECORDED	FEBRUARY 1993 MARCH–MAY 1993 DECEMBER 1993–MAY 1994
STUDIOS	OUT OF THE BLUE (MANCHESTER) REAL PEOPLE STUDIOS (LIVERPOOL) PINK MUSEUM (LIVERPOOL) MONNOW VALLEY STUDIO (WALES) SAWMILLS (CORNWALL) CLEAR (MANCHESTER) MATRIX (LONDON)
LENGTH	51:57
LABEL	CREATION
PRODUCERS	OWEN MORRIS OASIS MARK COYLE DAVID BATCHELOR
ARTWORK	

1994	CORN EXCHANGE / CAMBRIDGE, UK
1995	'LIVE FOREVER' VIDEO SHOOT / LONDON, UK #1 BORN IN MADCHESTER / SIMON SPENCE SAN FRANCISCO / CALIFORNIA, USA CLEVELAND / OHIO, USA DETROIT / MICHIGAN, USA SHEFFIELD ARENA / SHEFFIELD, UK GLASTONBURY FESTIVAL / SOMERSET, UK SLANE CASTLE / NEAR DUBLIN, IRELAND

MAYBE

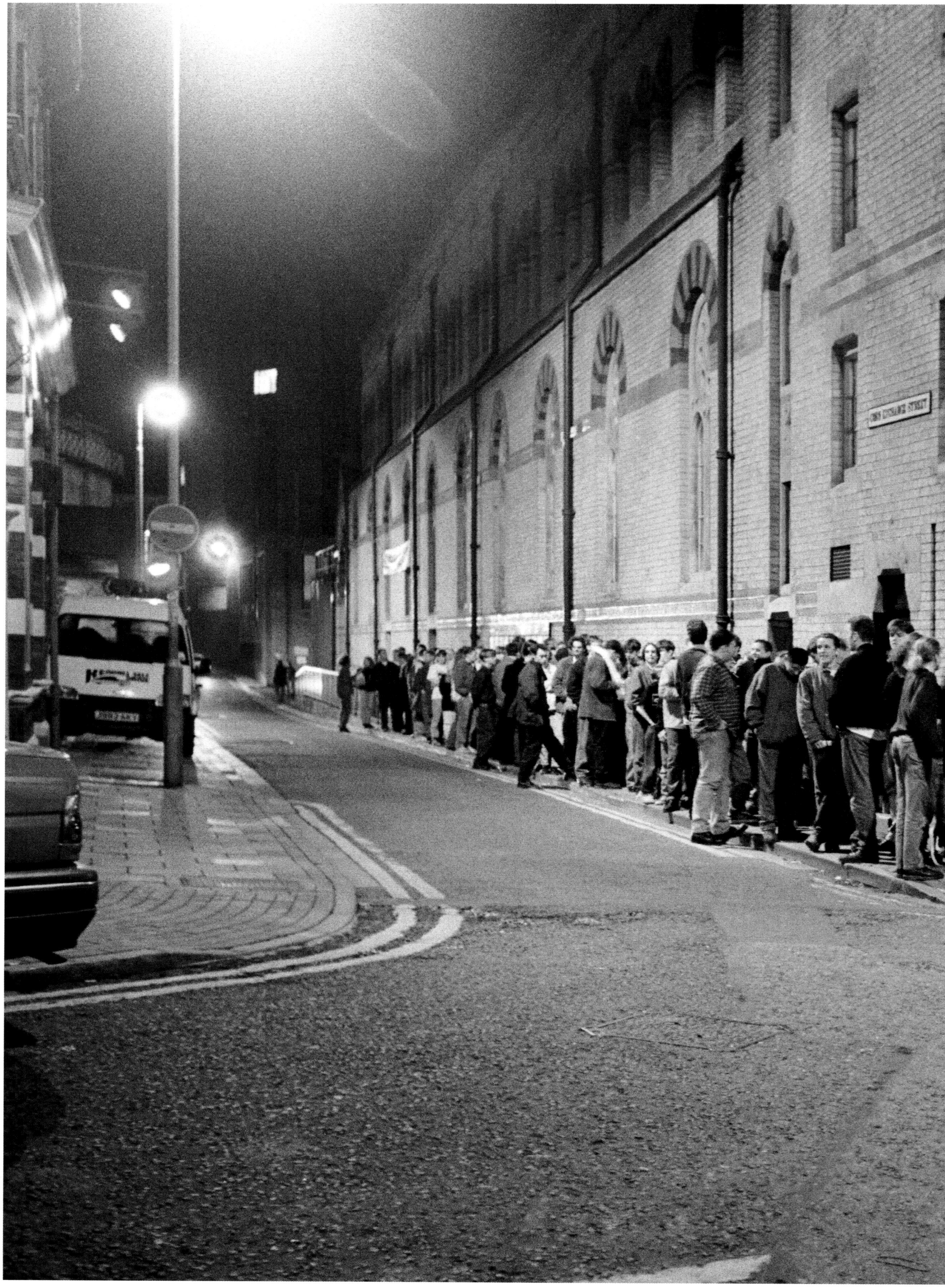

WHEELER STREET
Tourist
information
AIDA

THIS IS THE FUNNY THING. IN THE EARLY YEARS, IT WAS ALL GIRLS, REALLY. AND THEN THIS LADDISH THING. THEN THE GIRLS ALL STARTED TO MOVE A LITTLE BIT FURTHER BACK, AND THEN ALL OF A SUDDEN, YOU'RE JUST PLAYING TO A LOAD OF FUCKING GEEZERS. I DON'T CARE WHAT ANYONE SAYS. IT IS NOT AS MUCH FUN.

←← / ←

4 DECEMBER 1994
CORN EXCHANGE
CAMBRIDGE, UK

←← / ←

4 DECEMBER 1994
CORN EXCHANGE
CAMBRIDGE, UK

I REMEMBER THAT NIGHT VIVIDLY. THAT WAS A GREAT NIGHT. THAT'S KIND OF MY FAVOURITE PERIOD OF OASIS. THAT'S KIND OF WHERE THE CURVE STARTS GOING UP AND PHOTOGRAPHERS ARE SHOWING UP JUST TO SHOOT US.

4 DECEMBER 1994
CORN EXCHANGE
CAMBRIDGE, UK

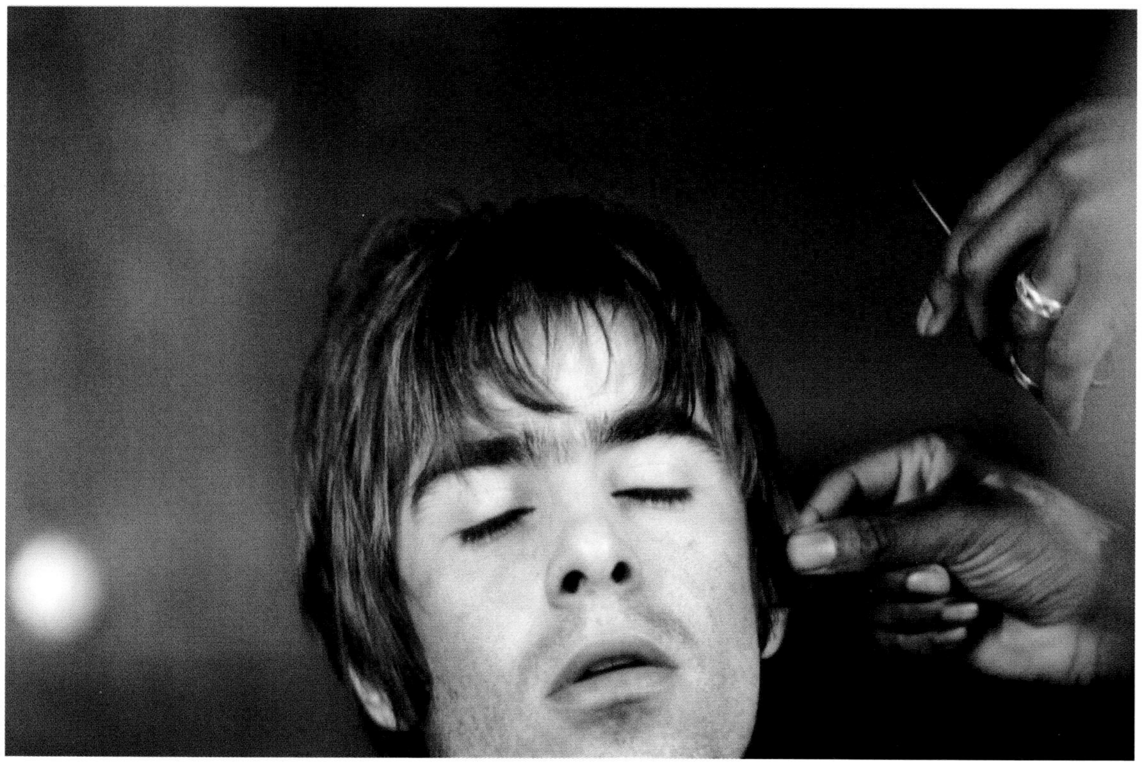

←→/→→

5 JANUARY 1995
'LIVE FOREVER' VIDEO SHOOT
PORTLAND PLACE, LONDON, UK

←→/→→

5 JANUARY 1995
'LIVE FOREVER' VIDEO SHOOT
PORTLAND PLACE, LONDON, UK

KODAK 5063 TX
KODAK 5063 TX
KODAK 5063 TX

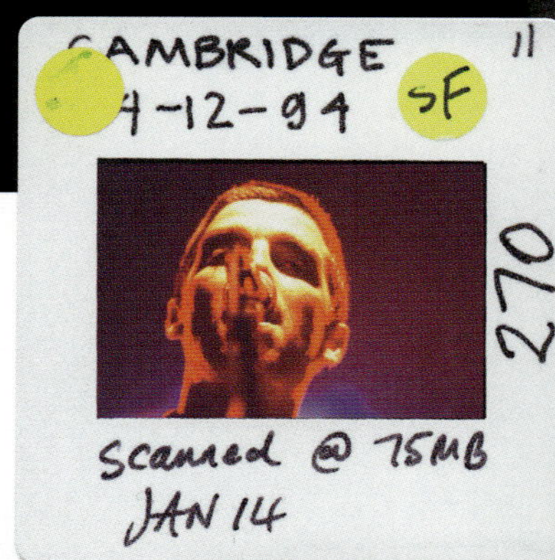
CAMBRIDGE
4-12-94
SF
11
270
Scanned @ 75MB
JAN 14

19
SF
Cambridge
4/12/94
OASIS
© JILL FURMANOVSKY
JFA ARCHIVE
8 FITZROY ROAD
337

TOILETS

KODAK 5063 TX

KODAK 5063 TX
KODAK 5063 TX
KODAK 5063 TX
oasis
oasis

#1 BORN IN MADCHESTER

SIMON SPENCE

Without the late eighties 'Madchester' explosion of music, fashion and clubbing, there would have been no Oasis. For Noel Gallagher, then in his early twenties, the world-leading, headline-grabbing scene happening in his home city of Manchester was a spiritual awakening. He'd been a roadie for Inspiral Carpets, set to be made famous by Madchester, but it was illegal acid house raves and nights at the city's infamous Haçienda club that transformed him.

'It was a social musical revolution, our generation's answer to punk,' he recalled. 'It was quite an incredible thing that just happened out of nothing.'

Noel's songwriting ambitions radically shifted. The influence of the decade's dominant Manchester band, The Smiths, downbeat and often insular, was replaced by wide-eyed, feel-good, unifying themes.

'I used to live right in the town centre, on the same street as the Haçienda, sitting in a flat all day smoking weed, playing the guitar. The sun would be shining and you'd go to the Haçienda at the weekend thinking, "This can't last forever, someone's going to put a stop to this. This is ridiculous." It was great. Really, really brilliant.'

Liam was also converted by Madchester. He loved electro music and hip-hop, and was a keen breakdancer, but acid house and raves in fields and abandoned warehouses were not his thing, and he was uninterested in guitar music. However, his chance attendance at a gig by pivotal Madchester band The Stone Roses changed his life. In the Roses, he saw a future for himself. A year zero.

Under their influence, he explored touchstone bands such as the Rolling Stones and the Sex Pistols, and became a disciple of the 'baggy' Madchester look, particularly the edgy, homegrown streetwear brand Gio-Goi. Full of swag 'n' blag, the famous Manchester 'front', Liam was persuaded to become the singer for Madchester wannabes The Rain, featuring three future Oasis band members, whose closest brush with fame at that point was attending the Stone Roses' epochal Spike Island event.

When the Madchester boom ended in 1992, and the world's media's attention was drawn to a new citadel and sound – Seattle and the emerging grunge scene led by Nirvana – The Rain were left floundering, with songs by Liam and the band's guitarist Paul 'Bonehead' Arthurs judged derivative and dated. They changed their name to Oasis, but their efforts were distinctly unrefreshing. The name was actually a misnomer. A visiting drug dealer had noted the lack of ambience in a band rehearsal and, asked for his thoughts, said dismissively, 'It's like an oasis in here.' He had meant the opposite – the atmosphere arid, without life. On the lookout for a new name, drummer Tony McCarroll had jumped on the comment.

Liam was twenty. Life stared him in the face. At five feet ten inches tall, he'd been cock of his school (meaning the best fighter in his year) and its blue-eyed heartthrob, with scores of girls knocking on his door daily. Now, like many of his pals – rogues, shoplifters and petty criminals, born afresh during the Madchester era but held fast by the ongoing socio-economic disintegration in the UK that arose during Margaret Thatcher's decade as prime minister – Liam was going nowhere, picking up work on building sites or as a valet cleaning the cars of Manchester United footballers.

Through clubbing and partying, Noel – almost six years Liam's elder – became a face in Manchester, pals with Johnny Marr and many others at the city's outrageous Factory Records. The brothers had drifted apart after Noel left home. The scars of a savage childhood were still raw. Their father was a gambler and drinker, a violent man who had regularly punched and kicked his wife and children. Noel got the worst of the beatings, developing a pronounced stammer that took four years of speech therapy to correct. At seventeen – sick, he said, of 'all the years of physical and mental abuse' – Noel booted his father out of their lives.

Liam was only twelve when this happened. He, despite everything, missed his father. Will, as he was known back then, short for William, was left rudderless. His mum, Peggy, went out to work at a biscuit factory and he sat on his own in front of the TV. The wall of machismo he erected around himself was protection from his loneliness and sadness; the hole his father left in his life made him crave attention and eat up the limelight. Bono said it was 'the ache' in Liam's voice that elevated Oasis into the rock stratosphere, and it was born of his innate fury and frustration.

'Life makes us who we are,' Liam told me in 1994. 'I'm glad of who I am. I wouldn't change anything in my life and a lot of bad things have happened. If we all came from Essex and our dad worked for British Aerospace and he had two Mercedes and he borrowed one to me every now and again, Oasis wouldn't exist.'

Noel had inherited his father's looks but Liam had his volatile temperament, enjoying the buzz of violence. An infamous incident in his final year at school saw three lads attack him; he was struck on the head with a hammer, blood everywhere, yet still Liam emerged victorious, knocking all the other kids out. 'When Liam loses it, it's scary,' said Owen Morris, the producer who helped shape the early Oasis sound. It became a band leitmotif.

31 JANUARY–2 FEBRUARY 1995
SAN FRANCISCO
CALIFORNIA, USA

Criticized by Keith Richards and George Harrison for his assiduous threats to 'fucking knock out' all-comers (such as Robbie Williams and Damon Albarn), Liam deadpanned, 'I will beat the fucking living daylights out of them.'

When he finally saw Liam's band play live, Noel – shrewd, calculating and possessed by a ferocious drive to succeed – saw a vehicle for his ambitions, the means of turning his new songs into hits. His takeover and remodelling of Oasis would involve a year of fractious rehearsals, poorly attended gigs and primitive recordings. The industrious Noel not only gave the band the songs that would form the bedrock of their debut album, he encouraged Liam towards Beatles records and books. John Lennon became a new touchstone for the singer.

Oasis was not all Noel's creation, however. One key signifier, which would go on to ignite and inform the mid-nineties Britpop scene, was already in place when he took over. Despite having a strong Irish heritage, the band was already using a Union Jack in its logo. 'The greatest flag in the world going down the shitter and we're here to do something about it,' Liam declared proudly. Soon, Noel's guitar would be famously decorated in the flag, as the era of Britpop and 'Cool Britannia' was born.

The building stones for becoming the most famous (and notorious) rock 'n' roll band in the world were already in place when Alan McGee chanced on Oasis playing bottom of the bill at a small gig at King Tut's in his home city of Glasgow in 1993. Famously, he signed them on the spot. In Liam and Noel, he recognized an alluring brothers-in-arms image, and beneath that the simmering sibling rivalry that would prove endlessly fascinating to the world. 'We disagree about everything,' Noel said. 'I write the music and the lyrics so it's like, "You sing that." He goes, "I'm not singing that." I'm like, "You're singing that or you're getting the sack."'

McGee, a master of hype, had already overseen the rise of two of the UK's most controversial acts, The Jesus and Mary Chain (featuring the infamous Reid brothers) and Primal Scream. His record label, Creation, was at the cutting edge of UK indie dance/rock, shoegaze and grunge, and McGee's reputation for hedonism was legendary.

Amplified to the nation, Oasis became an instant hit, an overnight sensation. The band's look and attitude had Madchester writ all over it. High-octane songs such as 'Rock 'n' Roll Star' and 'Cigarettes & Alcohol' were made incendiary by being deliberately, defiantly proletariat.

'We don't write about politics or anything like that per se,' Noel said. 'We write about how the dreams you have as children fade away, how shit it is leaving school and finding out life is a bag of shit. The only time we get angry is on the day of the general election and we get our polling card and go you fucking Tory bastards let's fucking have it and you put your cross in. That's it. Cos if we all vote together and we all vote Labour...it's like someone from the Redskins once said: If we all spit together, we drown the bastards.'

The brothers, as McGee had foreseen, proved to be a photographer's dream and countless journalists were left in thrall to their nothing-to-lose rock 'n' roll behaviour. Fights and arguments between Noel and Liam became a mainstay of almost every article written about them, alongside their passion for Man City football club. Infamy inflamed the wild side of Liam, the young meteorite. He trashed hotel rooms, gobbled drugs, banged groupies and was proud of it. He was the life and soul of the non-stop Oasis party, the young man dancing and singing on top of the tour bus wrapped in a Union Jack.

'They want the showman, they get the showman,' he said. 'But if they want the young northern upstart they can have that instead.' He adopted the term 'Mad For It' to describe his philosophy of life and bragged the lie that he'd never read a book. 'People think I'm just a fucking lunatic,' he declared.

Noel countered, 'We're not mad, we're just bored. If there was any bands or new music or fashion to get into, I'd be on it. But there's not so we're bored, so we end up fighting with each other. Oasis are bored shitless. We don't give a fuck.'

Liam's abrasive attitude and style – *his walk* – made him an icon for a generation, the nation's favourite bad boy. He inspired the popularity of nineties 'lad culture', from *Loaded* magazine to Damien Hirst, just as Noel's support for the Labour Party mobilized a new generation to vote for Tony Blair who was elected prime minister in 1997.

There were inevitable casualties. McCarroll was sacked (he was unable to 'live the dream,' said Liam); bassist Paul 'Guigs' McGuigan quit then rejoined the band after a nervous breakdown. Liam himself seemed on the brink of psychosis. Noel would say success made Liam 'more stupid' and called him 'out of control' and 'beyond therapy'. The band's manager, Marcus Russell, said he 'feared like fuck' for Liam.

The music was initially downplayed amid the melodrama. Of pissing-out-their-territory debut single 'Supersonic', Noel said, 'I lifted the guitar from "My Sweet Lord" by George Harrison. Bit cheeky that. It's not exactly the same but it's similar. I'm not an original songwriter. I listen to records and think that's alright but I can do it better.' A second single, 'Shakermaker', became the subject of a successful lawsuit from the writers of 'I'd Like to Teach the World to Sing (In Perfect Harmony)'.

'Live Forever' broke that mould, the first indication of the scale of what Oasis could achieve and their first Top 10 single. Rarely credited, this new CinemaScope version of the band bore the hallmarks of bassist Guigs's twin passions, Queen and country music – anthemic and heartfelt, the sort of thing, like the band's down-to-earth Mancunian wit and suss, you could never fake.

The release of 'Live Forever' foreshadowed the eleven-song *Definitely Maybe* album, a now timeless emblem of the era. Within a week of its release in August 1994 it was No.1, the fastest-selling debut album in UK history at the time.

Days later, on the road in the US, months into a slew of hectic live performances, Liam famously attacked Noel on stage at the end of a showcase gig in Los Angeles, reputedly while on a crystal meth binge. Noel briefly abandoned the US tour as headlines about the break-up of the band blazed. The live recording of the unhinged LA show is still extraordinary to listen to.

In the UK, the guitar scene coalesced around Oasis, with bands such as Blur, Pulp and Suede cast as support acts to this once-in-a-lifetime phenomenon.

'When we hear Liam's voice, it's our voice, it's everyone's voice,' said Pete Townshend. 'Live Forever', and the many hits that followed, would become everyone's songs and Oasis everyone's band.

STOP

31 JANUARY–2 FEBRUARY 1995
SAN FRANCISCO
CALIFORNIA, USA

STOP

31 JANUARY–2 FEBRUARY 1995
SAN FRANCISCO
CALIFORNIA, USA

I got to know the band much better on the stage and off when I went to San Francisco with them. Guigs and Bonehead were a great foil for Noel and Liam, and Tony McCarroll was good natured. The combination was highly entertaining. There was a lot of laughing on that trip, and I felt I could do something special with them.

31 JANUARY–2 FEBRUARY 1995
SAN FRANCISCO
CALIFORNIA, USA

PEOPLE SEE IT AS MINE AND LIAM'S BAND. IT'S ACTUALLY BONEHEAD'S BAND BECAUSE HE INVITED LIAM TO JOIN AND LIAM INVITED ME. BONEHEAD WAS THE ORIGINAL MEMBER. HE WOULD ALWAYS KNOCK OUR HEADS TOGETHER FOR THE SAKE OF THE BAND.

©F.X.
CATNIP

↑→

15 MARCH 1995
CLEVELAND, OHIO, USA

KODAK GPY
47
GPY
44
KODAK GPY
GPY 3
46
GPY 2
45
ROLLING ROCK
Budweiser
GPY 1
Scan
Nov 2010
081876

16 MARCH 1995
DETROIT
MICHIGAN, USA

PRIVATE
Operated By

BP

STOUFFER TOWER

16 MARCH 1995
DETROIT
MICHIGAN, USA

WE BLEW UP QUITE QUICKLY, BUT WE WERE STILL BOOKED IN TO PLAY ALL THESE PLACES THAT HAVE NO BARRIER. THE MUSIC WAS QUITE ENERGETIC ROCK 'N' ROLL, AND YEAH, I REMEMBER THERE BEING CRAZY FUCKING NIGHTS ON STAGE.

→ / →→

16 MARCH 1995
SAINT ANDREW'S HALL
DETROIT, MICHIGAN, USA

It was really tight and intense in there, and the band were not used to a mosh pit and people in the audience crowd surfing. The dressing room was cramped and had two doors – one leading to the stage and the other to an alley. Halfway through the set, Noel left the stage in need of a leak. I held open the door to the alley so he could reenter at speed. Liam announced to the audience that his brother had to take a piss.

adidas

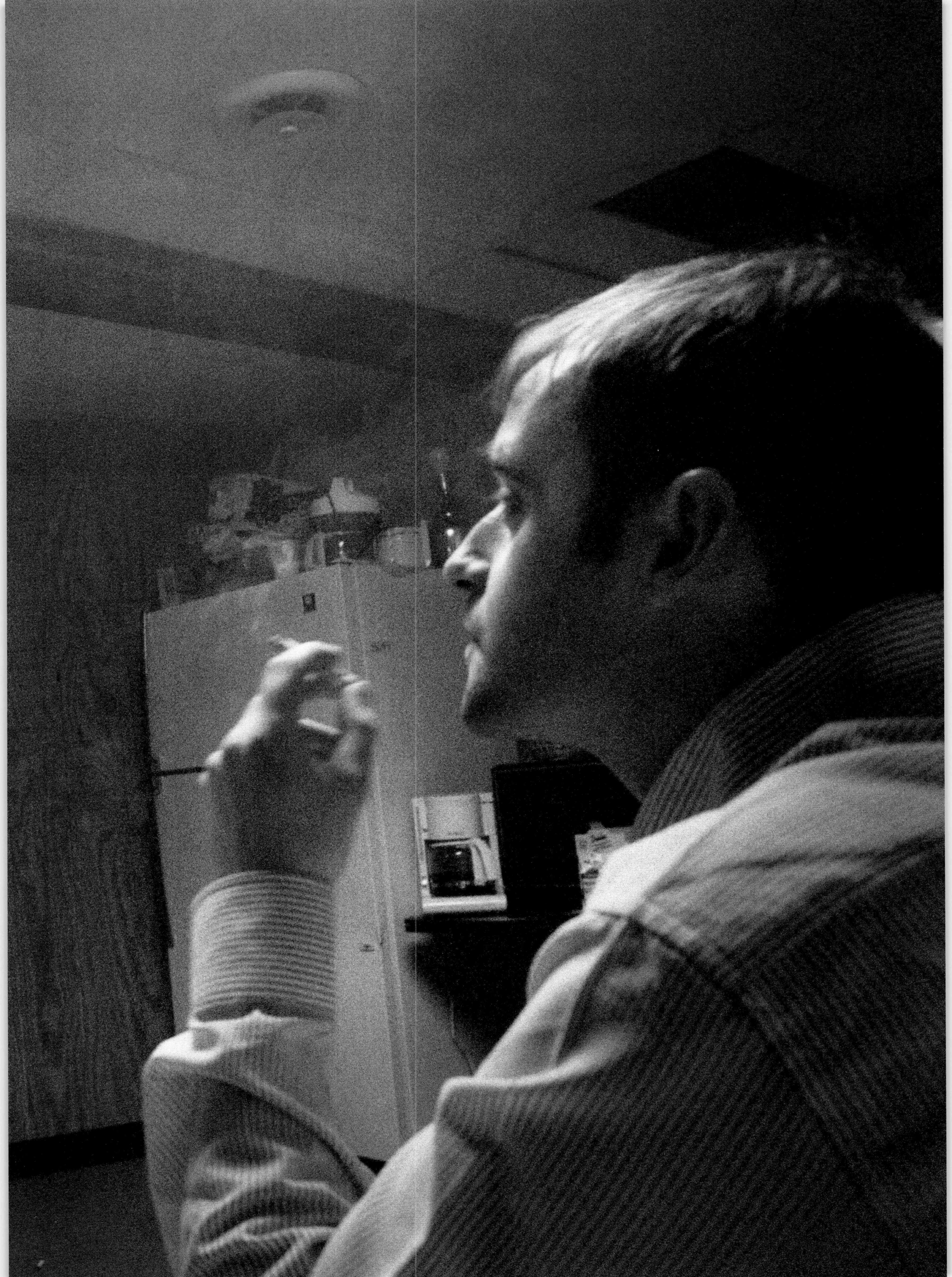

←

16 MARCH 1995
SAINT ANDREW'S HALL
DETROIT, MICHIGAN, USA

Noel with Maggie Mouzakitis, Oasis tour manager.

←

23 MARCH 1996
THE POINT
DUBLIN, IRELAND

Noel with his mother, Peggy, and two of her sisters in a nearby pub.

IF WE'D HAVE HAD A FELLA AS A TOUR MANAGER, I DON'T KNOW WHAT WOULD HAVE HAPPENED ON THE ROAD. BUT BECAUSE WE'D ALL KIND OF BEEN BROUGHT UP HEAVILY BY OUR MUMS – ALL OF US – SHE FUCKING RULED. SHE WAS FROM QUEENS IN NEW YORK. SHE WAS GREEK. I DO MISS HER. I FUCKING ADORE THAT WOMAN.

22 APRIL 1995
SHEFFIELD ARENA
SHEFFIELD, UK

This was one of the first big concerts Oasis gave, and the first time they played a large arena. When they walked onto the stage I think they were really quite overwhelmed that they had such a huge audience. I think you can see that in a couple of the shots.

Up to this point, they had played halls and smaller venues with audiences of only 2,000 or 3,000 people. Sheffield Arena is one of the largest indoor arenas in the UK and has a capacity of 13,600 – and the concert was completely sold out.

26 JUNE 1995
GLASTONBURY FESTIVAL
SOMERSET, UK

Co-creators of the Glastonbury Festival, Michael and Jean Eavis, join Oasis before their headline set.

22 JULY 1995
SLANE CASTLE
NEAR DUBLIN, IRELAND

The concert field within the grounds of Slane Castle provides a natural amphitheatre for an audience of up to 80,000 people. The River Boyne runs alongside it, and some of the fans donned wetsuits and swam across to get into the concert for free.

(WHAT'S THE STORY)

RELEASED	2 OCTOBER 1995
RECORDED	FEBRUARY 1995 MAY–JUNE 1995
STUDIO	LOCO STUDIOS (WALES) ROCKFIELD STUDIOS (WALES) ORINOCO STUDIOS (LONDON)
LENGTH	50:06
LABEL	CREATION
PRODUCERS	OWEN MORRIS NOEL GALLAGHER
ARTWORK	

1995 'WONDERWALL' VIDEO SHOOT / LONDON, UK
EARLS COURT / LONDON, UK
PARIS / FRANCE
CREATION PARTY / LONDON, UK

1996 US TOUR / PHILADELPHIA, PENNSYLVANIA, USA
US TOUR / RHODE ISLAND, USA
US TOUR / UPSTATE NEW YORK, NEW YORK, USA
THE POINT / DUBLIN, IRELAND
MAINE ROAD / MANCHESTER, UK
ROYAL FESTIVAL HALL / LONDON, UK
REHEARSALS, NEC / BIRMINGHAM, UK
BALLOCH CASTLE COUNTRY PARK / LOCH LOMOND, SCOTLAND
KNEBWORTH PARK / HERTFORDSHIRE, UK
PÁIRC UÍ CHAOIMH / CORK, IRELAND

MORNING GLORY?

THE MUSIC GENERATED A FEELING OF CAMARADERIE WITH THE PEOPLE THAT LISTENED TO IT. ALL ACCIDENTALLY. I COULDN'T TELL YOU WHAT I WAS TRYING TO ACHIEVE WHEN I WAS WRITING IT – I WAS JUST WRITING IT. THE BIG SONGS THAT WE ALL KNOW WERE WRITTEN WHEN I WASN'T EVEN A ROCK STAR. I WAS UNEMPLOYED, SO I WASN'T WRITING IT FROM THE PERSPECTIVE OF HAVING AN AUDIENCE OR ANYTHING. I WAS WRITING IT FOR ME. OUR MUSIC IS NOT MUSIC THAT KEEPS THE LISTENER ON THE OUTSIDE. IT INVOLVES THE LISTENER – IT REQUIRES THEM TO SING ALONG AND FEEL IT.

→

29 SEPTEMBER 1995
'WONDERWALL' VIDEO SHOOT
LONDON, UK

↓→

29 SEPTEMBER 1995
'WONDERWALL' VIDEO SHOOT
LONDON, UK

Scott McLeod, who briefly replaced Guigs as bass player, is the one sitting reading a newspaper in parts of the video.

29 SEPTEMBER 1995
'WONDERWALL' VIDEO SHOOT
LONDON, UK

Video sets are a great place to take set-up photos because you can take full advantage of the beautiful lighting. Here, the big lights created silhouettes of the figures. The 'Wonderwall' video was filmed by director Nigel Dick, and it went on to win British Video of the Year at the 1996 BRIT Awards.

KODAK TX 6043
125362

EARLS
oasis

COURT
oasis

Velocifero

I'D BEEN ON HOLIDAY IN ITALY. I REMEMBER BEING OUT ONE NIGHT AND SEEING THESE KIDS WHIZZING BY ON THESE SCOOTERS. I CAN'T REMEMBER WHAT THEY WERE CALLED NOW. I REMEMBER FINDING OUT WHERE THE SHOP WAS AND THINKING, I'M GOING TO BUY ONE OF THOSE FOR EACH OF THE BAND. WE WERE RIDING AROUND THE VENUE ON THEM, SPEEDING AROUND THE BACK.

←← / ←

4–5 NOVEMBER 1995
EARLS COURT
LONDON, UK

4–5 NOVEMBER 1995
EARLS COURT
LONDON, UK

Noel and Liam never stood together and sang into the same microphone and they certainly never put their arms around each other on stage. When he wasn't singing Liam would prowl around the stage, so the only way to get both of them in one picture during a performance was to take a photo when one walked past the other, usually from the side of the stage. I was always on the lookout for that moment. It often ended up being the shot used on the record or video cover.

PARIS IS QUITE A SIGNIFICANT PLACE IN THE TALE OF OASIS. WE DID SOME REALLY AMAZING GIGS THERE BUT WE ALSO HAD SOME CATASTROPHIC DAYS AND NIGHTS THERE. IT'S WHERE I WROTE 'DON'T LOOK BACK IN ANGER' AND IT'S ALSO WHERE THE BAND BROKE UP.

→

23 NOVEMBER 1995
PARIS, FRANCE

↑→

23 NOVEMBER 1995
PARIS, FRANCE

Diesel Dynamics

WE JUST LOOK SO UNINTERESTED IN BEING THERE. I REMEMBER LIAM BEING ABSOLUTELY RAT-ARSED AND BEING IN A PROPER FUCKING BAD MOOD. AS YOU CAN SEE, WE'VE DRESSED UP SPECIFICALLY FOR THE OCCASION TO HAVE OUR PICTURE TAKEN ON THAT BRIDGE IN PARIS. IT LOOKS LIKE WE'VE JUST WALKED OFF A BUILDING SITE. EVERY TIME I SEE THAT PICTURE, I CAN SEE FROM MY FACE I'M JUST SAYING, 'JILL, I SWEAR TO GOD, IF YOU DON'T FUCKING HURRY UP....' BECAUSE, AS YOU KNOW, I DON'T LIKE HAVING MY PICTURE TAKEN AT THE BEST OF TIMES.

← / →→

23 NOVEMBER 1995
PARIS, FRANCE

23 NOVEMBER 1995
PARIS, FRANCE

For the shoot in Paris, we were all supposed to meet in Noel's hotel room at around 10:30, then go out to take the shots. We had two mini-buses booked to drive us around. So, everybody was there, hanging out in Noel's room, apart from Liam. While we were waiting for him, I took some shots of Noel and the rest of the band on the balcony, which spectacularly overlooked the Place de l'Opéra. It transpired that Liam had been in the hotel bar all night and was still there. My assistant persuaded him to leave, and we all set off towards the river. Noel was furious by this time. When we got there, Liam hurtled around, wine glass in hand, greeting passersby at random. I suggested that Noel stand on a bridge and wait for Liam to join. It was a bit like when Liam was roaming around on stage and I was waiting for them to come into the same frame. When Liam arrived, I shot off a reel of film of the two of them. Later we did some classic band shots on the banks of the Seine. Liam lay under a tree for a while – well, he hadn't been to bed yet.

ON THAT FUCKING NIGHT, CREATION WERE HAVING A PARTY FOR US. I ARRIVED LATE, AND THAT ROLLS ROYCE WAS PARKED OUTSIDE. THEY GOT ALL THE BAND VINTAGE ROLEXES, REALLY FUCKING NICE WATCHES, PROBABLY WORTH MORE THAN THE CAR NOW. I WAS LAST TO GET CALLED UP. THEY SAID, 'WE HAVEN'T GOT YOU A WATCH.' AND I WAS LIKE, 'IS THAT MY CAR OUTSIDE?' AND THEY SAID, 'WELL, YEAH, IT IS.' AND FUCKING LIAM'S FACE! HE GOT A WATCH, HE THOUGHT, AND I GOT A CAR...! I STILL CAN'T DRIVE TO THIS DAY. I DON'T EVEN KNOW WHAT HAPPENED TO THAT CAR.

←

22 DECEMBER 1995
CREATION PARTY
LONDON, UK

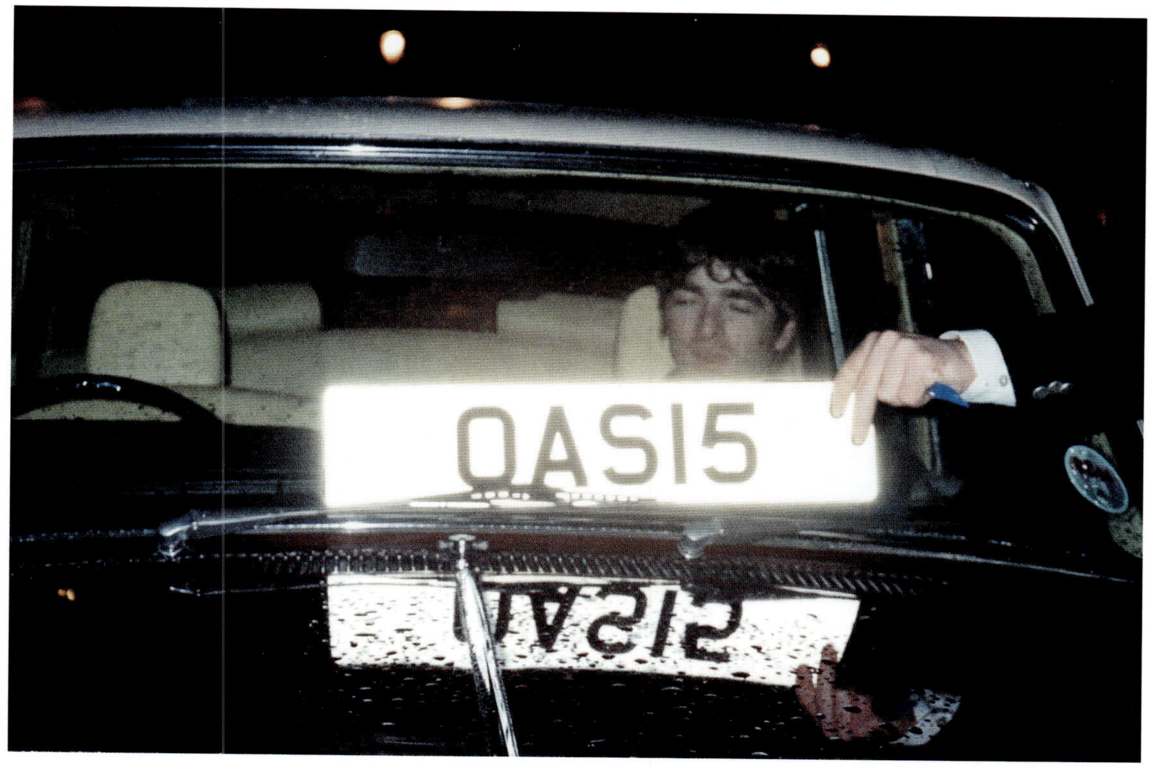

←→

22 DECEMBER 1995
CREATION PARTY
LONDON, UK

Liam and Noel appraise their Christmas gifts during the party, which was also attended by Emily Eavis (top left).

tower
TONITE
OASIS
THE GEFKENS
ONE WAY

oasis
WE GOT POT

←

9 MARCH 1996
US TOUR, PHILADELPHIA
PENNSYLVANIA, USA

'WE GOT POT.' YEAH, IF EVER A BAND WAS NOT FUCKING WEED SMOKING, IT WAS OASIS. THAT AIN'T GOING TO GET YOU BACKSTAGE AT AN OASIS GIG. IF YOU SAID, 'WE'VE GOT COCAINE,' WE'D HAVE BEEN LIKE, 'RIGHT, GET THEM IN!'

9–10 MARCH 1996
US TOUR, PHILADELPHIA
PENNSYLVANIA, USA

Because the distances between venues are so great on a US tour, many bands tend to sleep one night on the tour bus and the next in a hotel. My bunk was opposite Liam's on the bus. I saw he was asleep in his cubicle and thought I'd try to get a shot of him. I was afraid he might wake up when the flash went off, but luckily he didn't stir.

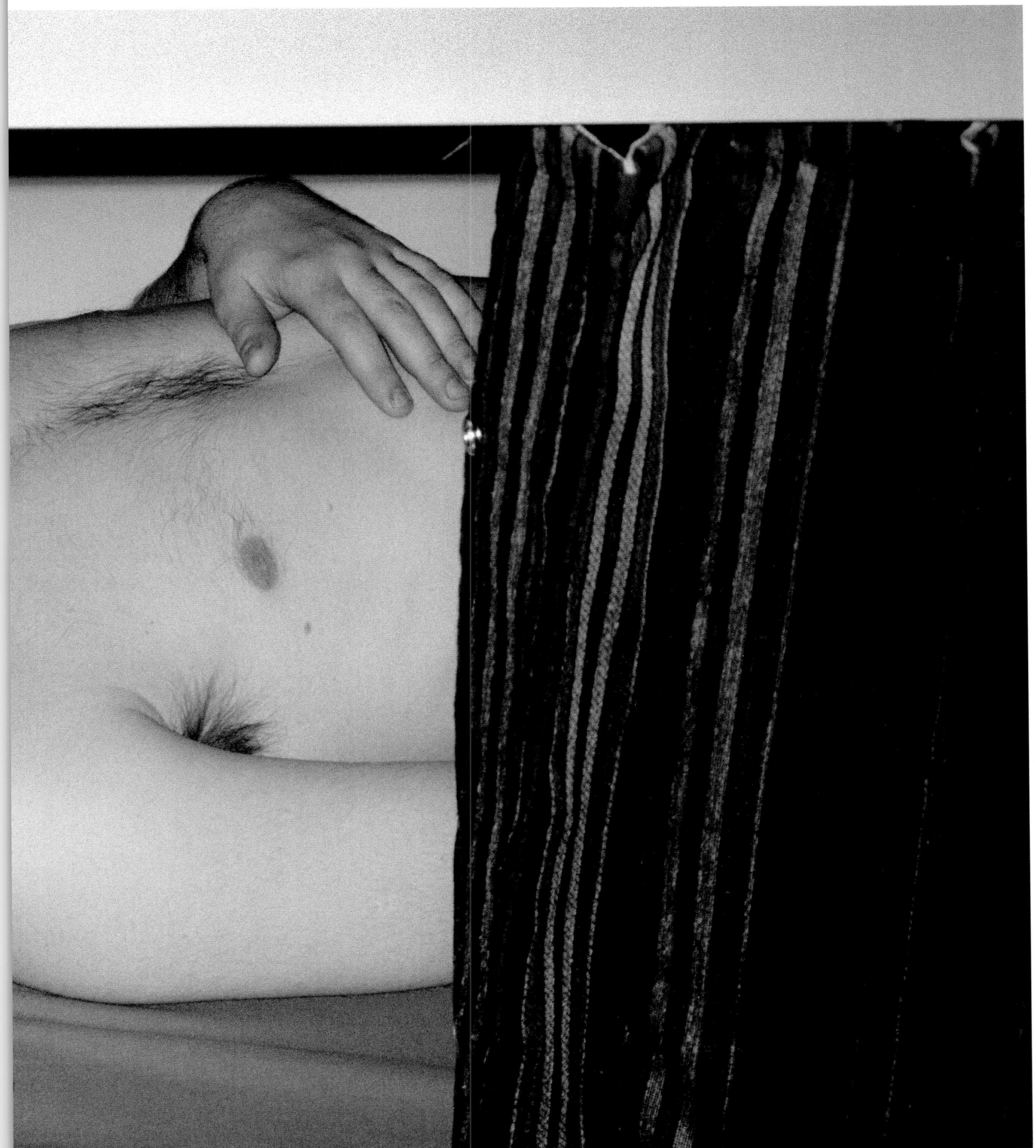

THE COAT THAT NEVER CAME OFF. FOR ABOUT A YEAR AND A HALF, LIAM WORE IT ON STAGE AND OFF. AND, AS FAR AS I KNOW, FOR THAT TOUR, IT DIDN'T GO TO THE DRY CLEANER'S OR ANYTHING. IT PROBABLY JUST WENT IN THE BIN AT THE END OF THE TOUR. THAT COAT IS ON EVERY SINGLE PICTURE FROM THAT TOUR.... YEAH...I BET IT STUNK.

→ / →→

10 MARCH 1996
US TOUR
RHODE ISLAND, USA

A4
A6

A18

12–13 MARCH 1996
US TOUR, UPSTATE NEW YORK
NEW YORK, USA

At the time, Noel did all the interviews, press and live radio broadcasts, usually on his own. On this occasion, he was asked to go upstate into the Catskill Mountains to play a song for a radio station there. There was a lot of snow on the ground and the temperature was well below zero. Noel had only a thin parka with him. Playing in front of a small crowd of people in their ski gear, his fingers almost froze to the frets of his guitar. The man sleeping beside Noel in the limousine is his bodyguard, Kevin.

←← / ←→

23 MARCH 1996
THE POINT
DUBLIN, IRELAND

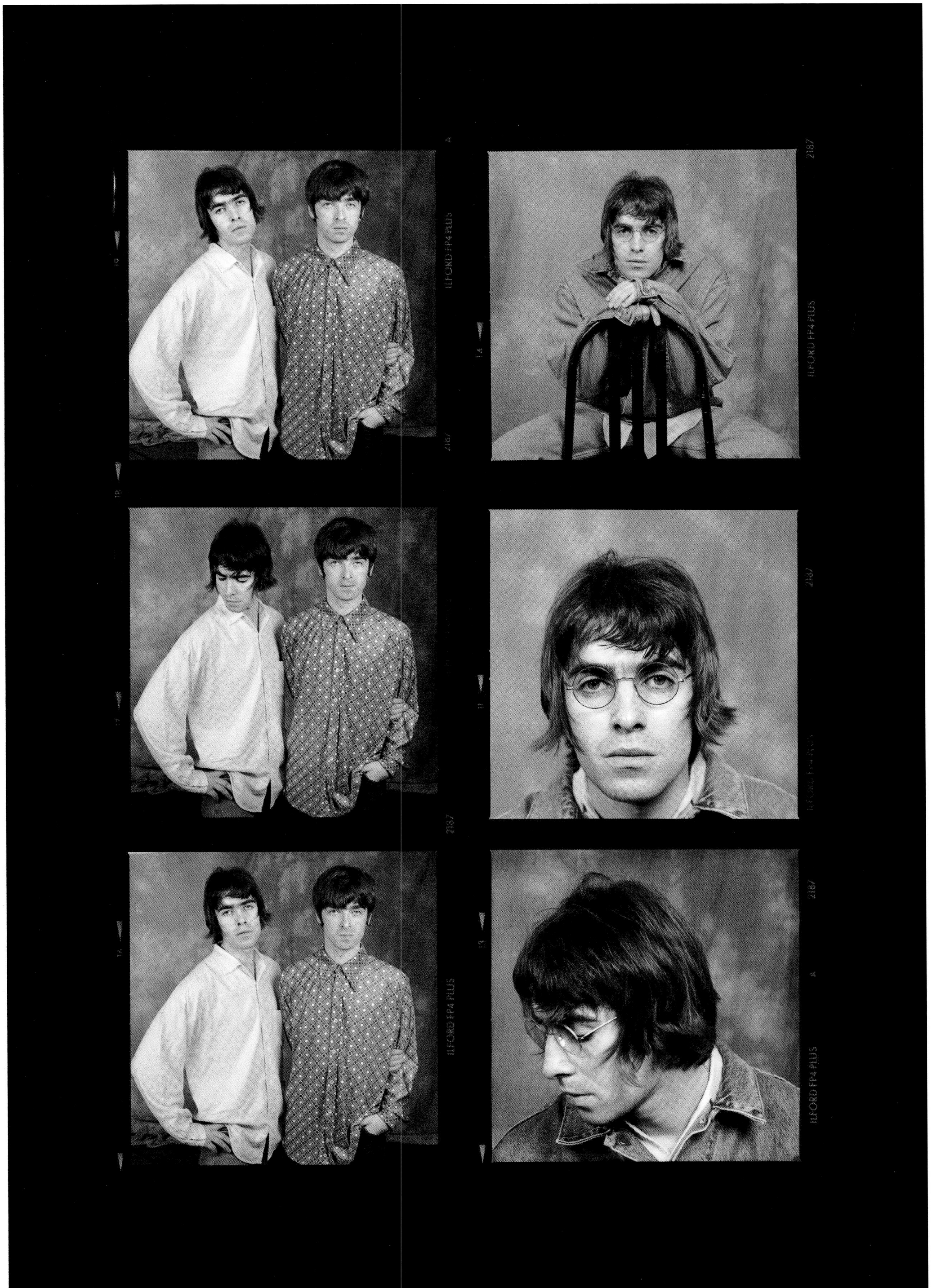
ILFORD FP4 PLUS
2187

CLASSIC
TRAVEL WRIGHT
KEEP CLEAR
EXIT

JEFFS

UMBRO
M.&W. FREIGHT LTD.
PRESSPART
Lloyds Metal Group plc
DEBORAH SERVICES
01924 378222
makro

THE INCREDIBLE THING ABOUT THIS BEING IN 1996 IS WE ONLY GOT A RECORD DEAL IN 1994, SO WE'D GONE FROM NOTHING TO THIS IN ABOUT EIGHTEEN MONTHS. THAT WAS OUR FIRST EVER STADIUM GIG. THE SHOT [OVERLEAF] TELLS THE STORY OF THE CONNECTION BETWEEN THE BAND AND THE AUDIENCE. THE PICTURE SAYS TO ME THAT EVERYBODY WHO'S IN THAT STADIUM IS WITH US, YOU KNOW, HEART AND SOUL, AND WE HADN'T PLAYED A NOTE. LOOK AT THAT! WE HADN'T PLAYED A SINGLE NOTE. WE'D NOT EVEN PLUGGED IN TO PLAY. LOOK AT THAT REACTION! BANDS WAIT TWENTY YEARS FOR THAT SHIT AND NEVER GET IT.

←← / ← / →→

26–28 APRIL 1996
MAINE ROAD
MANCHESTER, UK

EXIT

UMBRO

26–28 APRIL 1996
MAINE ROAD
MANCHESTER, UK

oasis

I WAS IN A HOTEL IN SANTA MONICA. MY EYE WAS DRAWN TO THIS GUY WHO WAS IN RECEPTION. SO, I GOT UP AND WENT OVER TO HIM. I WAS LIKE, 'ARE YOU BURT BACHARACH?' HE SAT TALKING TO US AND WAS TELLING ME THAT HE WAS GOING TO LONDON TO PLAY HIS FIRST EVER UK SHOW. I SAID, 'WHO'S GOING TO SING "THIS GUY'S IN LOVE WITH YOU"?' WHICH IS ONE OF MY FAVOURITE SONGS. AND HE SAID, 'WHY DON'T YOU COME AND DO IT?' AND TO CUT A VERY LONG, AMAZING STORY SHORT, JILL CAME WITH ME, AND WE ALL ENDED UP IN HIS DRESSING ROOM.

→

28 JUNE 1996
ROYAL FESTIVAL HALL
LONDON, UK

Kate Moss and Noel with Burt Bacharach in his dressing room at the Royal Festival Hall, London, and Noel accompanying Burt on stage.

28–29 JULY 1996
REHEARSALS, NEC
BIRMINGHAM, UK

oasis

Marshall
Marshall

4 AUGUST 1996
BALLOCH CASTLE COUNTRY PARK
LOCH LOMOND, SCOTLAND

→→

10–11 AUGUST 1996
KNEBWORTH PARK
HERTFORDSHIRE, UK

THAT WAS THE SUMMER OF BIGNESS. WE SPENT IT ON HELICOPTERS FLYING AROUND, PLAYING THE BIGGEST PLACES THAT EVER WERE. YOU KNOW, WE WERE THE BIGGEST THING SINCE SLICED CHEESE.

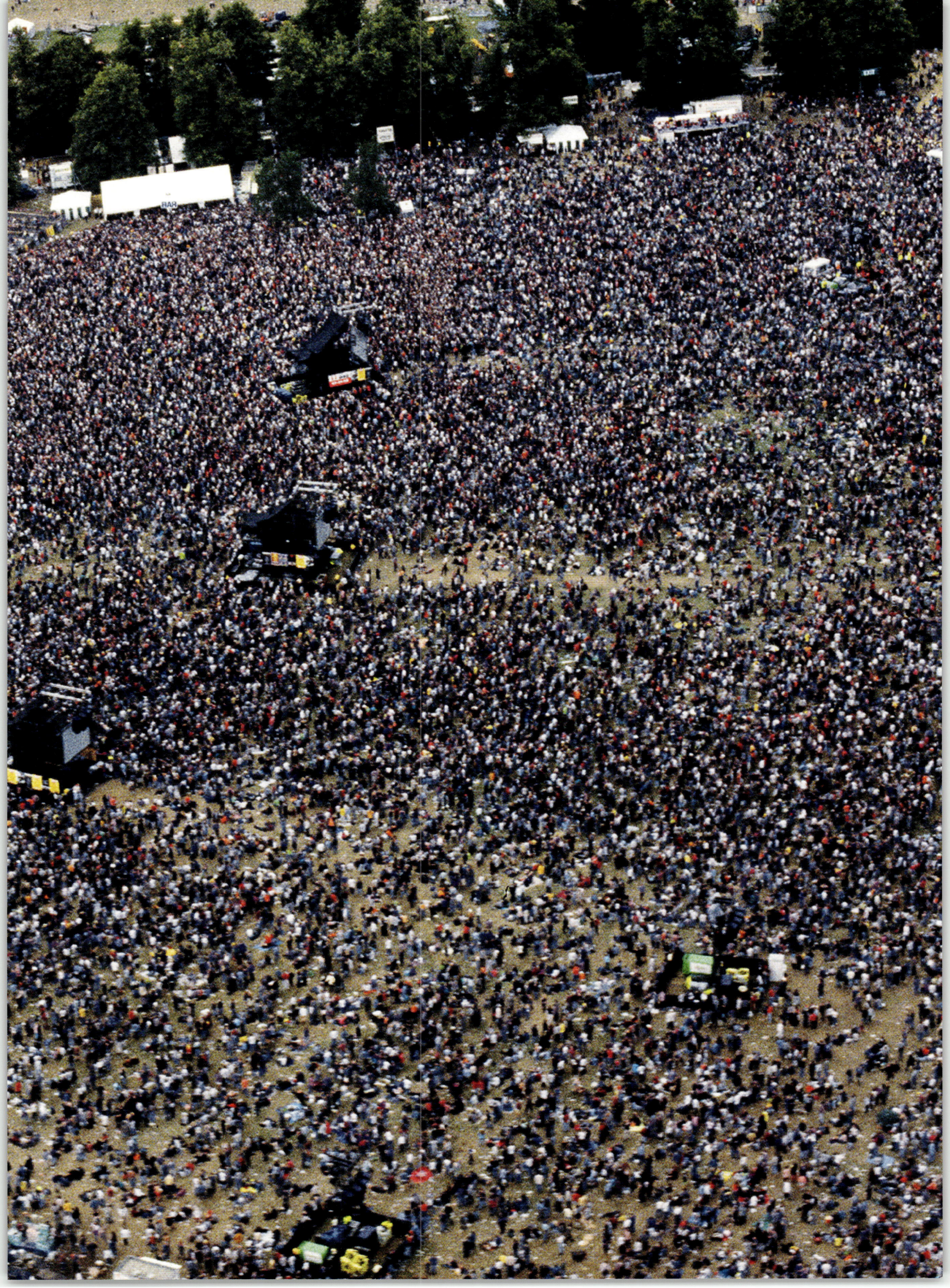

BEFORE WE WENT ON FOR ONE OF THE BIGGEST GIGS OF ALL TIME, THERE WAS NO KIND OF BAND HUDDLE. I HAD A CIG, LIAM HAD A BEER. SOMEONE CAME IN AND SAID, ‘RIGHT, THAT’S IT.’ WE JUST WALKED ON STAGE AND DID IT, AND THEN CAME OFF STAGE. THERE WAS NO ‘RIGHT, EVERYBODY OUT, WE NEED TO PRAY.’

←← / → / →→

10–11 AUGUST 1996
KNEBWORTH PARK
HERTFORDSHIRE, UK

The two shows at Knebworth were the last that Noel and I remember that were free of mobile phones, and so they had great intimacy. On stage on the second night, Liam borrowed his fiancée Patsy Kensit’s oversized cream Aran sweater. Perhaps not the most suitable garment for a summer’s night performing under hot lights. But somehow it worked and those images of him have become iconic. This is another ‘crossing shot’ I was always on the lookout for: Noel tethered to his guitar and amp, and Liam cruising past him.

DAF

14–15 AUGUST 1996
PÁIRC UÍ CHAOIMH
CORK, IRELAND

There was a particularly lively atmosphere at the stadium in Cork. The audience were all on top of one another, excited and energetic, joining in and singing every song: an Irish audience supporting an Irish band. The crowd were part of the show.

BE HERE NOW

1996	ABBEY ROAD / LONDON, UK THE WARRINGTON / LONDON, UK RIDGE FARM STUDIO / SURREY, UK #2 TRIUMPH AND TURBULENCE / JOHNNY HOPKINS
1997	AIR STUDIOS / LONDON, UK BOXING RING / WIGAN, UK HOLOGRAM STUDIO / LONDON, UK KING'S CROSS / LONDON, UK MUSIC BANK / LONDON, UK OAKLAND / SAN FRANCISCO, CALIFORNIA, USA EARLS COURT / LONDON, UK SCHIPHOL AIRPORT / AMSTERDAM, NETHERLANDS FESTHALLE / FRANKFURT, GERMANY SEC CENTRE / GLASGOW, SCOTLAND WEMBLEY ARENA / LONDON, UK

RELEASED	21 AUGUST 1997
RECORDED	NOVEMBER 1996–APRIL 1997
STUDIOS	ABBEY ROAD (LONDON) RIDGE FARM STUDIO (SURREY) AIR STUDIOS (LONDON) MASTER ROCK (LONDON) ORINOCO STUDIOS (LONDON)
LENGTH	71:31
LABEL	CREATION
PRODUCERS	OWEN MORRIS NOEL GALLAGHER
ARTWORK	

Noel had gone missing in the middle of the US tour and, for a short period, no one knew his location or that of the band. Tabloid photographer Dave Benett, who lived next door to me at the time, thought I was concealing them in my flat. He kept looking over the fence and asking, ‘Have you got them in there?’ When Noel and the band eventually resurfaced, I had to take a shot of them at Abbey Road Studios to show that the band was still together. They then went on to record *Be Here Now*.

FIRE EXIT

OCTOBER–NOVEMBER 1996
ABBEY ROAD
LONDON, UK

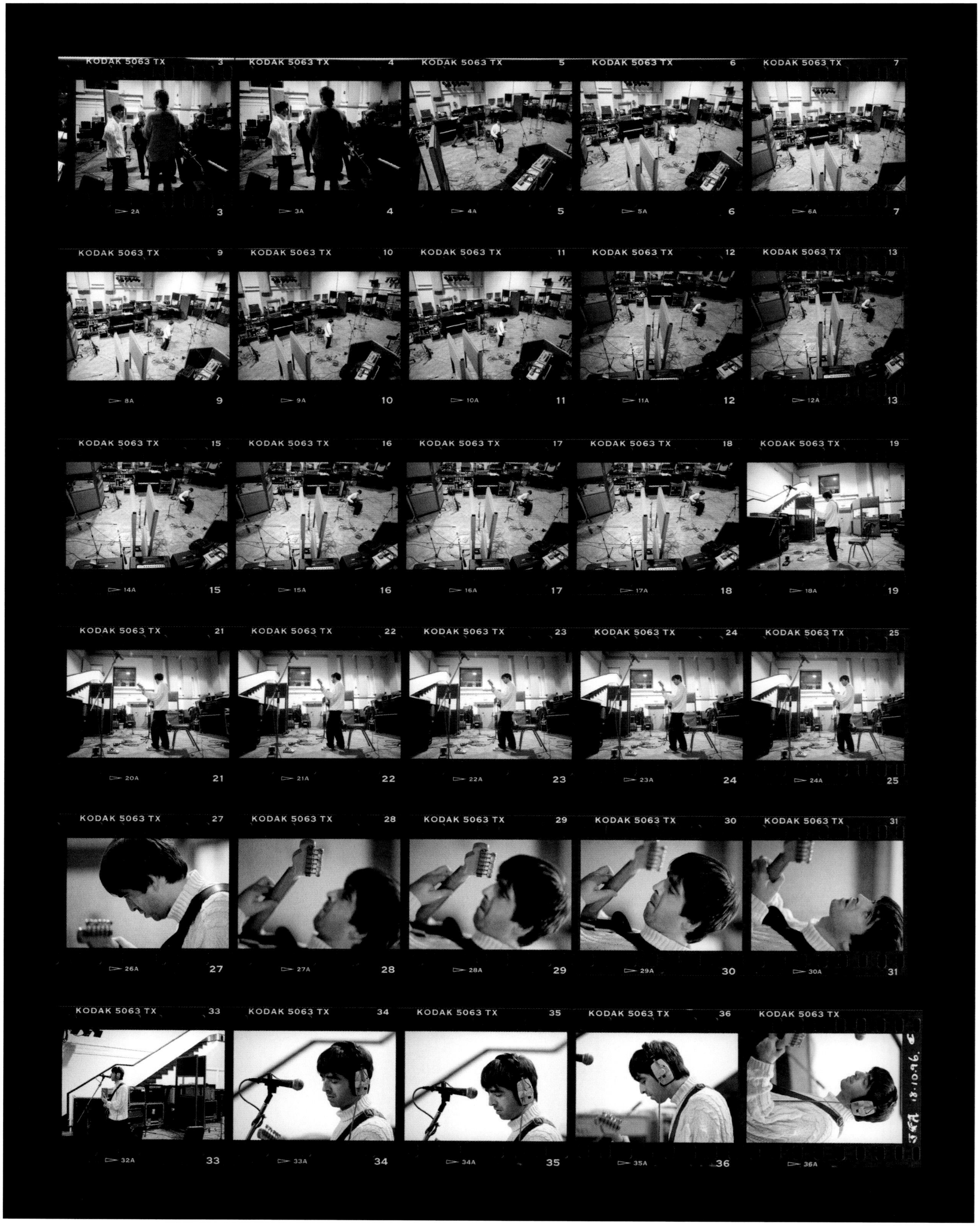

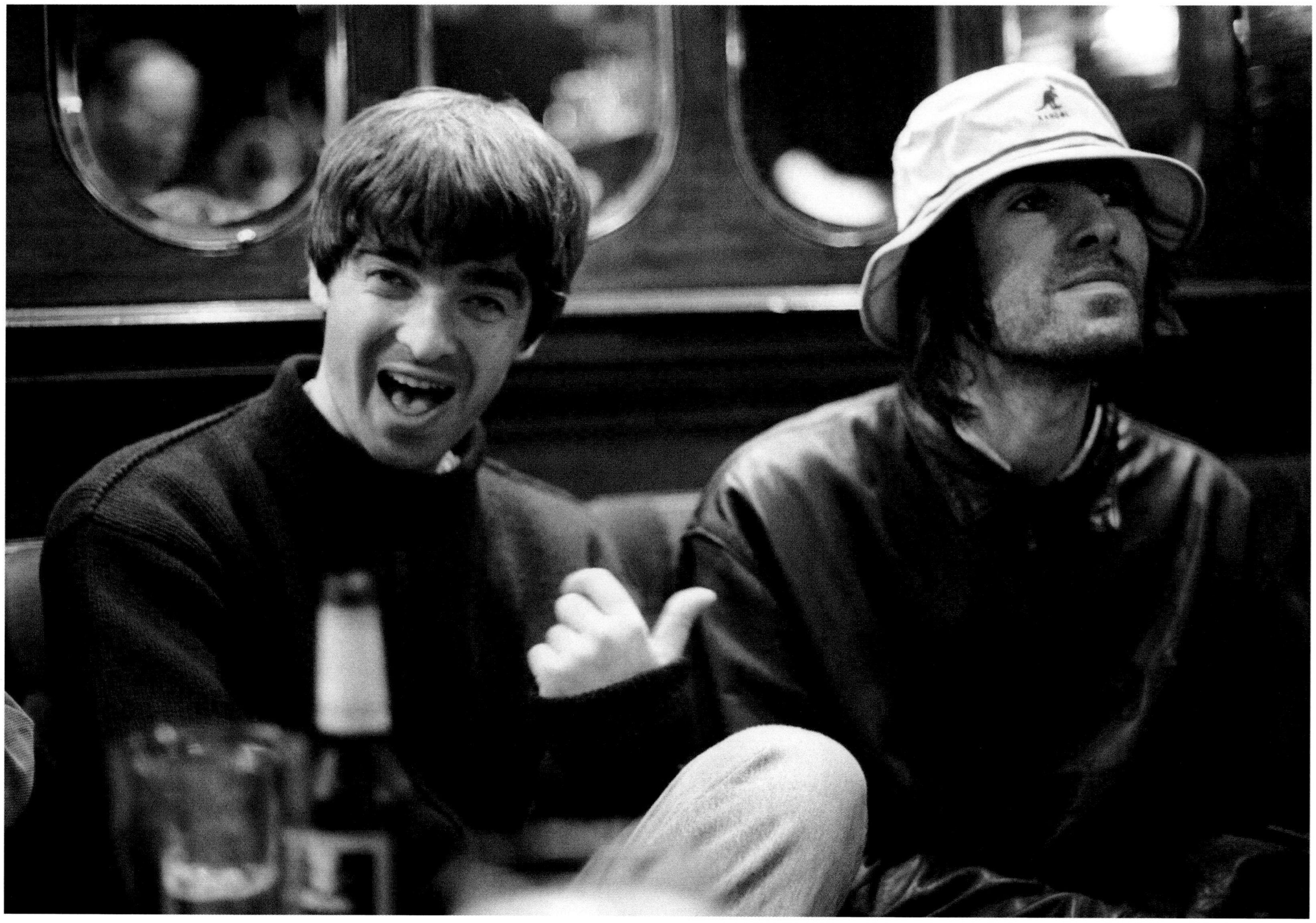

WE'D WON EVERYTHING AT THE MTV AWARDS, AND THE CEREMONY WAS TAKING PLACE IN LONDON. BUT THE FUNNY THING IS, WE FINISHED IN THE STUDIO AND WE WENT TO THE PUB FOR A DRINK. AND THEN WE JUST STAYED IN THE PUB AND NEVER WENT TO THE AWARDS. SEEING THE FOOTAGE BACK, THERE'S FIVE EMPTY SEATS AT THE FRONT DURING THE ENTIRE CEREMONY. THEY'D OBVIOUSLY CHOREOGRAPHED WHAT WAS GOING TO HAPPEN THAT NIGHT, AND EVERY TIME WE WON AN AWARD, IT WAS FIVE EMPTY SEATS. WE WERE IN THE PUB.

←

OCTOBER–NOVEMBER 1996
THE WARRINGTON
LONDON, UK

→→

NOVEMBER–DECEMBER 1996
RIDGE FARM STUDIO
SURREY, UK

oasis

oasis
KODAK GPX
OASIS.
Johnny Hopkins 6
© JILL FURMANOVSKY
JFA ARCHIVE
8 FITZROY ROAD
LONDON NW1 8TY
KODAK 5063 TX
KODAK 5028 VPH-2

#2 TRIUMPH AND TURBULENCE JOHNNY HOPKINS

The story of Oasis is the stuff of rock 'n' roll dreams. The sheer speed of their all-conquering journey still amazes me. Through 1994, they achieved critical acclaim, multiple magazine covers, a rabid fanbase and the fastest selling debut album to date. How much bigger could they be? The years 1995 to 1998 mark the peak of their extreme success. There were, inevitably, bumps in the road, too. Triumph and turbulence. As their PR at Creation in the nineties, I saw it all first-hand.

When you work with a band, you usually have a checklist of attributes that you hope the musicians have inherently, or can develop quickly: quality songs, captivating live shows, a strong image, engaging interviews and ambition. Few groups have all these in place at the start. Oasis did. They combined a rock star aura with a down-to-earth everyman appeal. Despite their fame, they could as easily be snapped nipping out for a packet of fags and a newspaper as attending an A-list party or award ceremony.

Oasis started out as a bunch of friends from the network of working-class Irish communities in South Manchester. Their individual personalities and the dynamics between them were crucial to their success. Liam was nicknamed the 'Tasmanian Devil', always a non-stop swirl of energy and movement. He had, and still has, the voice, the presence and the looks of a rock 'n' roll singer, as well as the ability to wear clothing from M&S and Next and make it look like hip and expensive designer gear. Throw in the sense of mischief and humour that ran through his psychedelic shaggy dog stories and you have an ideal star.

Not for nothing was Noel called 'the Chief'. He had a creative vision as well as a (master)plan for success, and he was determined to make it happen. Even while he was touring (and partying) around the world as a roadie for Inspiral Carpets, he was perpetually learning, writing and waiting for his own opportunity to come. When it did, his prolific songwriting could finally be appreciated. His insightful and funny interviews captivated media and fans.

Bonehead could play many, often contrasting, roles, from peace-maker to mischief-maker. As a skilled musician, his rhythm guitar work delivered an important layer to the dense Oasis sound, and he sometimes also contributed accordion and keyboards. He even had his own dedicated group of fans – Bonehead's Barmy Army.

Within the maelstrom around the band in the nineties, Guigs exuded a chilled wisdom. He was a deep thinker and voracious reader with an impressive knowledge of music, football, politics and more or less anything. A great bass player, a big reggae fan and a talented footballer who learnt from George Best, his dad's mate.

As the original drummer, Tony delivered a raw punk energy. This was shown to great effect on early tours, when Oasis encored with an extended cover of the Beatles 'I Am the Walrus', towards the end of which the band exited the stage one by one, leaving Tony to pound out the rhythm for a couple of minutes as the climax of the set. His replacement, Alan White, was already an experienced musician when he joined. He made the move to Oasis look easy, performing 'Some Might Say' on *Top of the Pops* on his first day. His second Oasis gig was headlining Glastonbury.

For all their reputation as party animals, one of things that stood out about Oasis was their incredible work ethic. My indispensable colleagues Vanessa Cotton, Tones Sansom and I saw and appreciated the hard graft that Oasis put into writing, recording, touring, doing press, radio and television to get where they wanted to go. Like Manchester City's Erling Haaland and Rodri, Oasis's work rate was immense.

If 1994 was a whirlwind for Oasis, 1995 to 1998 was a series of full-on tornadoes. Looking ahead to the *(What's the Story) Morning Glory?* campaign, I was keen to commission a female photographer as I'd noticed that the band worked productively with women, who drew out different sides of their personalities. A conversation about this with journalist Daniela Soave led her to suggest Jill Furmanovsky. It was arranged that Jill would come to experience Oasis live in Cambridge on 4 December 1994. She loved them, taking pictures that night that document their performance and growing fanbase. No one knew then that this was the beginning of a more than thirty-year working relationship between her and the band members.

The band continued their UK tour until 30 December 1994, finishing at Middlesbrough Town Hall. After a couple of weeks off, they were straight into their second US tour. From there, the schedule was relentless for the next two years. In late January, Jill and I headed to San Francisco to take a range of publicity photographs. The pictures are glorious, with Jill making creative use of the quality of light and the interesting perspectives offered by the steep, hilly streets of San Francisco. All that, plus Oasis headlined the legendary Fillmore, where The Who, Pink Floyd, Jimi Hendrix, Aretha Franklin and San Fran bands like Jefferson Airplane played landmark shows. Jill captured the band on the cusp of superstardom.

Late April saw a typically hectic week in which Oasis recorded a *Top of the Pops* performance, played Southend's Cliffs Pavilion, Paris's Le Bataclan and Sheffield Arena – and swapped Tony for Alan. Just a year after their first single, 'Some Might Say' became their first No.1 and Sheffield Arena their first stadium concert. That night they debuted 'Don't Look Back in Anger', which Noel had apparently written only a few days earlier. Further landmark gigs followed shortly after, including their first Glastonbury headline. The night before, I took a bunch of journalists to see their warm-up at Bath Pavilion – one of the best performances I'd ever seen. We watched with Ride's Andy Bell, who would become Oasis's bassist four years later.

Having steered the band away from media coverage that pigeonholed them with bands that were labelled as Britpop, the unwanted chart battle (and class war) with Blur dragged Oasis into that sphere. Sure, it made both bands bigger, but they would have achieved that success anyway. This face-off also turned them into daily fixtures in the tabloids, selling many papers along the way. The chart battle even made BBC television's *News at Ten*. The media were, of course, a key part of the band's success. From 1995 to 1998, Oasis featured on the cover of more or less every newspaper and magazine several times over. If 1993 to 1994 was about negotiating them into the papers, from 1995 the job was frequently about negotiating them out. The demand for interviews with the band was off the scale, not just in the UK but across the world. If they had done them all, they would not have had time to write and record new songs and play gigs, let alone sleep and eat.

2 MAY 1997
KING'S CROSS
LONDON, UK

In the midst of the *What's the Story* campaign, Oasis found time to record material for War Child's *HELP* album. This was to support children caught up in the Bosnian war that followed the break-up of Yugoslavia. As well as Oasis re-recording 'Fade Away', Noel got to collaborate with two of his heroes – Paul McCartney and Paul Weller – on a version of the Beatles' 'Come Together'. Relentless schedules, touring, the rapid arc of success and the attendant pressures can be unforgiving. So it was sad, if unsurprising, to see Guigs briefly leave the band in September, citing 'nervous exhaustion'. The band was not the same without him.

By this point, every day was a tornado. On Sunday, 1 October, after reading rave reviews for *What's the Story* in the press, we celebrated with breakfast at the album launch party, organized by Meg Mathews (Noel's then-girlfriend), in a grand Victorian townhouse in Kensington, with a massive Oasis ice sculpture and a string quartet playing songs from the album. A proud moment for Noel and Liam's wonderful mum Peggy. Then, we zigzagged across London, first to the Parkway pub in Camden to watch Liverpool versus Manchester United, featuring the return of Eric Cantona, then on to the Heavenly Social with the Chemical Brothers and Richard Fearless (of Death In Vegas) on the decks. Topped off with a dishevelled but entertaining midnight performance at Oxford Street's Virgin Megastore.

The next day, Oasis opened their UK tour. To borrow a football analogy, they proved that they could deliver on a rainy night in Stoke – and every other city. Reviewing the Stoke gig, *NME*'s Andy Richardson stated that, despite suffering some summer challenges, Oasis were the best band in the UK. Within a week, they were the biggest band too, as *What's the Story* went straight to No.1, selling 345,000 copies in the UK in its first week – a record-breaking amount. The album stayed at the top of the charts for ten weeks, eventually selling more than 25 million copies worldwide. The tour wound its way around the world, and Jill's pictures record key moments. Her session with the band in Paris, in November 1995, reveals the mischief and strain of this period. In the group photo, the Gallaghers stare in opposite directions, their faces interlocking like a rock- star yin and yang – differing forces, yet dependent on each other and fundamentally part of the same whole.

Released on 30 October, 'Wonderwall' shows the strength of Noel's songwriting. It inspired countless cover versions across different genres, including by Bring Me The Horizon, One Direction, Cat Power, LeAnn Rimes, Ryan Adams and thousands of buskers, as well as many samples used in hip-hop. Even the kitsch The Mike Flowers Pops version reached No.2. 'Don't Look Back in Anger' delivered Oasis another No.1 in February 1996.

The phenomenal success of *What's the Story* led to a series of massive gigs alongside their normal world tours. Just a year-and-a-half after their first single, they headlined two sold-out shows at Earls Court, at the time the biggest indoor concerts ever in the UK, causing a near earthquake, certified by the British Geological Survey as a 'seismic event'. Earls Court marked the spectacular return of Guigs; his replacement, Scott McLeod, had quit after a month in the middle of the US tour. These gigs were followed by two sold-out shows at Maine Road, the home of Noel and Liam's beloved Man City. All this culminated in a record-breaking pair of shows at Knebworth – 2.5 million people applied for 250,000 tickets. The scale of the shows is clear from Jill's panoramic photo. There were, allegedly, 7,000 people on the guest list for Creation's hospitality tent.

The phrase 'Cool Britannia' gained currency in 1996, initially through the US media. It encompassed a perceived golden age in the creative industries, the rise of Tony Blair's New Labour and Euro 96. The Conservatives and New Labour argued over ownership of the phrase, leading to a debate in Parliament. Cool Britannia was a cultural *moment*, a marketing buzzword, an illusion, exploited by politicians to win votes and by the media to sell magazines. While Oasis and their songs were genuinely uplifting, the concept of Cool Britannia was problematic, exerting a pervasive influence that, among other things, reduced politics down to image and celebrity. Within the Oasis camp, we treated it with suspicion. During a 1996 BRIT Awards acceptance speech, Noel praised Tony Blair, his bandmates and Alan McGee as sources of hope. In May 1997, New Labour won the general election by a landslide, in part due to the support from Noel and other creatives. Such was Noel's status and publicity value that Blair invited him to a party at 10 Downing Street on 30 July. An unprecedented accolade for a controversial rock star. Noel allegedly drew a Hitler moustache on a photograph of Margaret Thatcher.

Between Maine Road and Knebworth, Noel had found time to demo tracks for *Be Here Now* while holidaying at Mick Jagger's house in Mustique. The album was then recorded with Owen Morris at Abbey Road, Ridge Farm, Master Rock, AIR and Orinoco studios. I first heard the album in its entirety, along with members of the Oasis team, around the table in the grand pop art dining room at Noel's north London home Supernova Heights, with 'Stand by Me', 'My Big Mouth' and 'D'You Know What I Mean?' grabbing the attention. The latter kicked off the *Be Here Now* campaign with another No.1 hit. Following an extraordinary set of glowing reviews, the album landed on 21 August. It became the fastest-selling album of all time in the UK, selling more than 660,000 copies in just three days – nearly double the figure of its predecessor.

Little over a week later, the death of Princess Diana in a car crash while being chased by press photographers raised questions about tabloid intrusion. Diana's death significantly changed the mood of the country overnight. It seemed paralyzed in the moment. People turned inward, seeking solace in reflective, downbeat music such as Elton John's 'Candle in the Wind'. The reception of *Be Here Now* started to suffer as a consequence, although subsequent singles succeeded ('Stand by Me', No.2; 'All Around the World', No.1).

The *Be Here Now* stadium tour started in California in June 1997 with stage design based largely on the album sleeve, giving it a Spinal Tap feel. Luckily, no one got stuck in the phone box. The tour travelled around the world, ending with two sensational arena shows in Mexico City in March 1998.

After countless magazines and newspaper covers, TV and radio appearances, over 230 gigs, seven UK singles (four No.1s, three No.2s), two albums (both No.1s) and a shed full of awards (including four BRITS) in little over three years, Oasis had definitely earnt some time off the rock 'n' roll treadmill. But what would the band do on their return?

I used to bat . . . at No 10
WEST END FINAL
Evening Standard
DAD IS PM
The Blair family moves into Downing Street as Major quits leadership after massacre at polls

←→ / →→

FEBRUARY 1997
AIR STUDIOS
LONDON, UK

←←

FEBRUARY 1997
AIR STUDIOS
LONDON, UK

Patsy Kensit and Liam and Meg Mathews and Noel during a break in recording.

←

FEBRUARY 1997
AIR STUDIOS
LONDON, UK

After meeting Noel, George Martin commented, 'I consider Noel Gallagher to be the finest songwriter of his generation.'

GEORGE MARTIN WAS DOING A SERIES OR A DOCUMENTARY ABOUT BANDS LIKE US, AND WE HAD TO BE ON IT. HE MADE ME SHOW HIM HOW I WROTE 'WONDERWALL'. I'VE GOT TO SAY, OUT OF ALL THE EXPERIENCES I'VE HAD MEETING FAMOUS PEOPLE, THAT WAS THE MOST PETRIFYING BECAUSE HE WAS LIKE, 'CAN YOU GET A GUITAR AND SHOW US HOW YOU WROTE IT?' AND I WAS LIKE, 'ER....' HE DIDN'T EXPRESS THAT HE KNEW I WAS AN ABSOLUTE FUCKING CHANCER.

19 MARCH 1997
BOXING RING
WIGAN, UK

↓

1 MAY 1997
HOLOGRAM STUDIO
KINGSTON, LONDON, UK

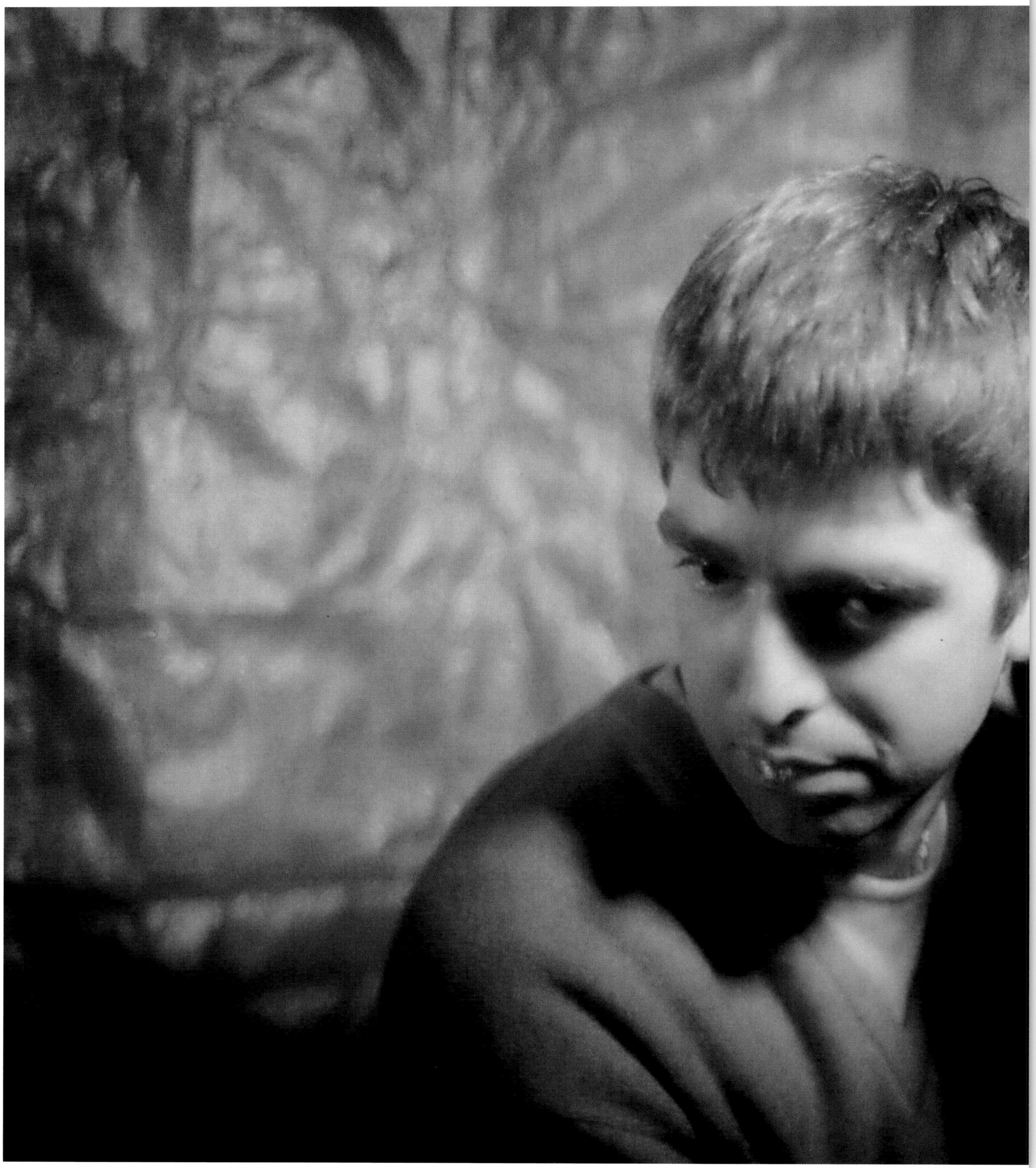

This is a photograph of a real hologram made with technical help from the renowned artist Chris Levine and his team. It was like a photoshoot but with a device that captured a 3D image using a number of lenses. I made this and a series of other holograms to show at my first Oasis exhibition 'Was There Then' (title made up on the spot by Noel to complement *Be Here Now*). The exhibition began at the Roundhouse in London in September 1997, then travelled to the Haçienda in Manchester and the Tramway in Glasgow, before ending up in Dublin's Gallery of Photography. When Noel saw one of the holograms of Liam he said, 'It's so real I want to hit it!'

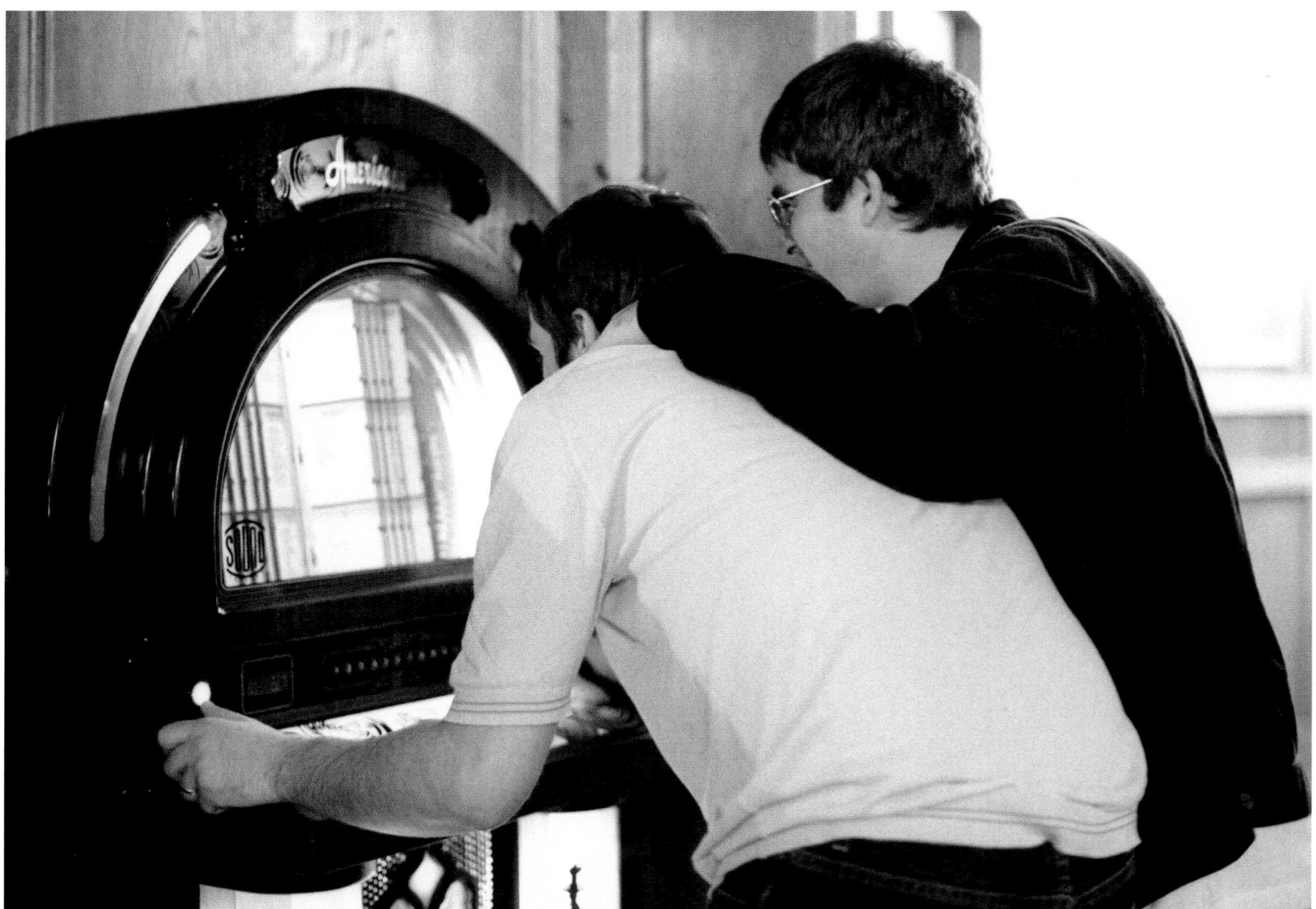

←→ / →→
2 MAY 1997
KING'S CROSS
LONDON, UK

For the second day of the shoot for *Be Here Now*, we hired a pool and snooker club in King's Cross, complete with bar and dartboard. Noel, Liam and 'Whitey' each wrote something on the blackboard about themselves. It was the day after the general election, and Tony Blair had just been elected prime minister. There was widespread euphoria across the country as people celebrated a change of government. The band were certainly celebrating. I ran out of film during the shoot and ordered some more. A motorbike messenger duly arrived with the film and did a double take when he saw Oasis sitting in the bar area. He was so shocked. The band thought it was hilarious.

THE BEST THERE WAS
THE BEST THERE IS AND,
THE BEST THERE EVER
WILL BE!

↑→

2 MAY 1997
KING'S CROSS
LONDON, UK

These images were the last of the two-day shoot. They were a write-off because everyone was hammered from a long session with an open bar in the pool and snooker hall. But, oh what fun we had....

↑→

28 MAY 1997
MUSIC BANK
LONDON, UK

FIRE EXIT

←→

18 JUNE 1997
OAKLAND
SAN FRANCISCO
CALIFORNIA, USA

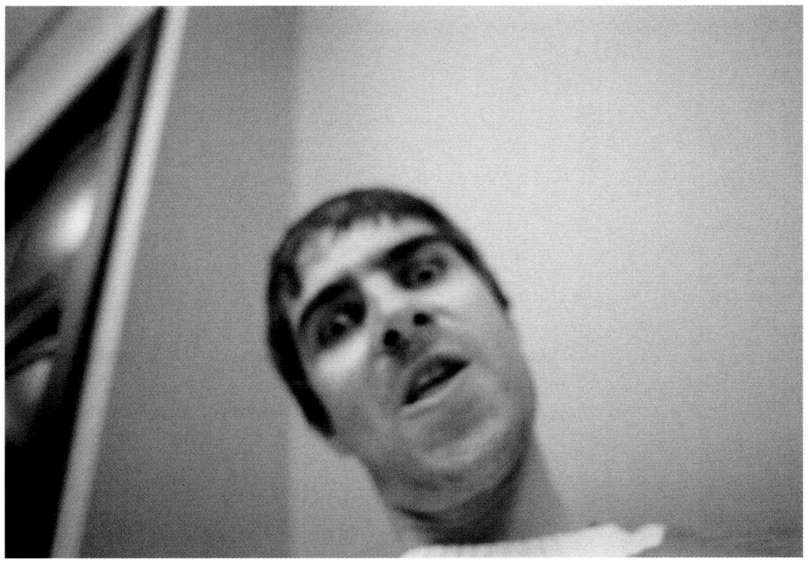

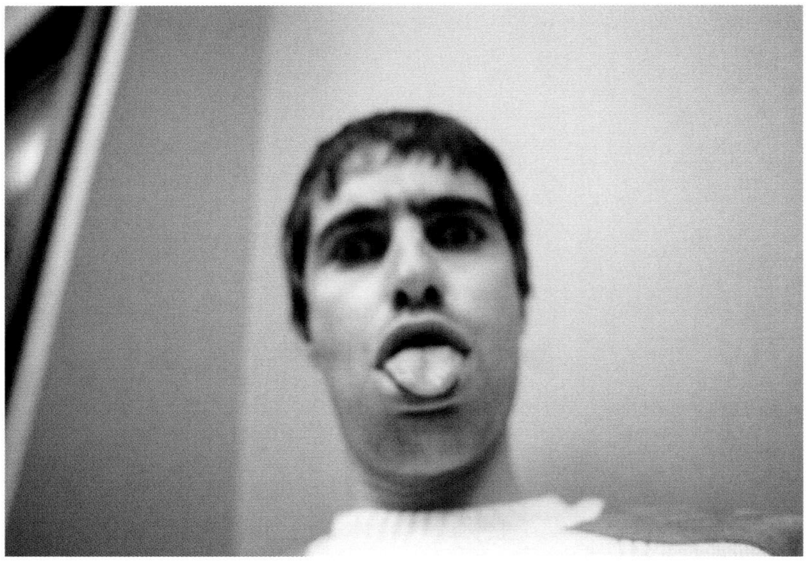

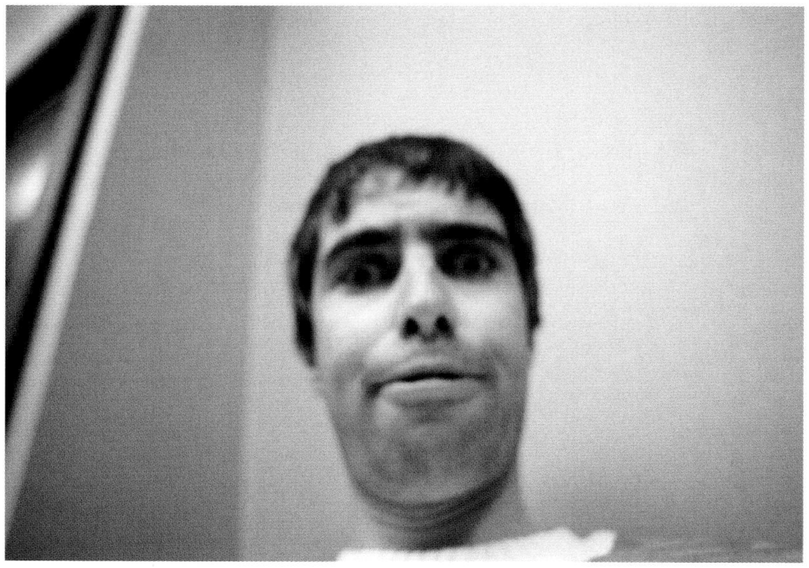

←

18 JUNE 1997
OAKLAND, SAN FRANCISCO
CALIFORNIA, USA

I took many photos of the band relaxing and mucking about in the dressing room at the Oakland Coliseum where they were opening for U2 on their *PopMart* tour. Afterwards, when I had the film processed, I discovered a whole series of shots of Liam that I definitely had not taken. He must have grabbed my camera at some point to take some selfies. He did a brilliant job of getting his head in the middle of each frame. And the inner workings of his mind come through loud and direct in every shot. Awesome.

→→

18 JUNE 1997
OAKLAND, SAN FRANCISCO
CALIFORNIA, USA

Liam was sitting in the wings while Noel sang 'Don't Look Back In Anger'. I had no idea who the figure was that loomed up behind him, but I changed focus quickly and realized it was Bono.

LIAM'S BECOME MORE MAD. HE'S TOTALLY FUCKIN' MENTAL. HE LIVES IN THIS WEIRD / BIZARRE-BIZARRE CONCEPT. I LOVE THE GEEZER. AND I DON'T SAY THAT JUST BECAUSE HE'S MY BROTHER. HE MAKES ME LAUGH. HE'S SO SURREAL.

AIR STUDIOS / EARLS COURT
LONDON, UK

I shot these portraits of Noel and Liam at AIR Studios in February 1997. Fans will recognize these images from the cover of my first Oasis book, *Was There Then*, designed by graphic design maestro Neville Brody. The same crop of each portrait was used on billboards for the band's shows at Earls Court, September 1997 (overleaf).

EARLS
oasis

COURT
oasis

25 NOVEMBER 1997
SCHIPHOL AIRPORT
AMSTERDAM, NETHERLANDS

→→→

25 NOVEMBER 1997
FESTHALLE
FRANKFURT, GERMANY

THE ERA OF US JUST BEING PISSED ALL THE TIME. FUCKING BRILLIANT. AND THE FOUNDER OF OASIS – BONEHEAD – PUT HIMSELF ON THE LUGGAGE CONVEYOR BELT.

adidas
Kappa

←↓/→→/→→→

7–8 DECEMBER 1997
SEC CENTRE
GLASGOW, SCOTLAND

The audience was mostly composed of teenage boys, who were enjoying an illicit beer or two before the gig. Once the show started, everything was fine until about halfway through, when a bottle was thrown at the stage. Bonehead immediately put down his guitar and walked over to Liam, who announced that they would not stand for it. The band promptly marched off stage. The audience erupted in anger. Windows were broken as dustbins and bottles were thrown around. Barricaded in the dressing room, we listened to the rampaging teenagers, who refused to leave. They hoped that the band would relent and go back on stage, but they didn't.

17–18 DECEMBER 1997
WEMBLEY ARENA
LONDON, UK

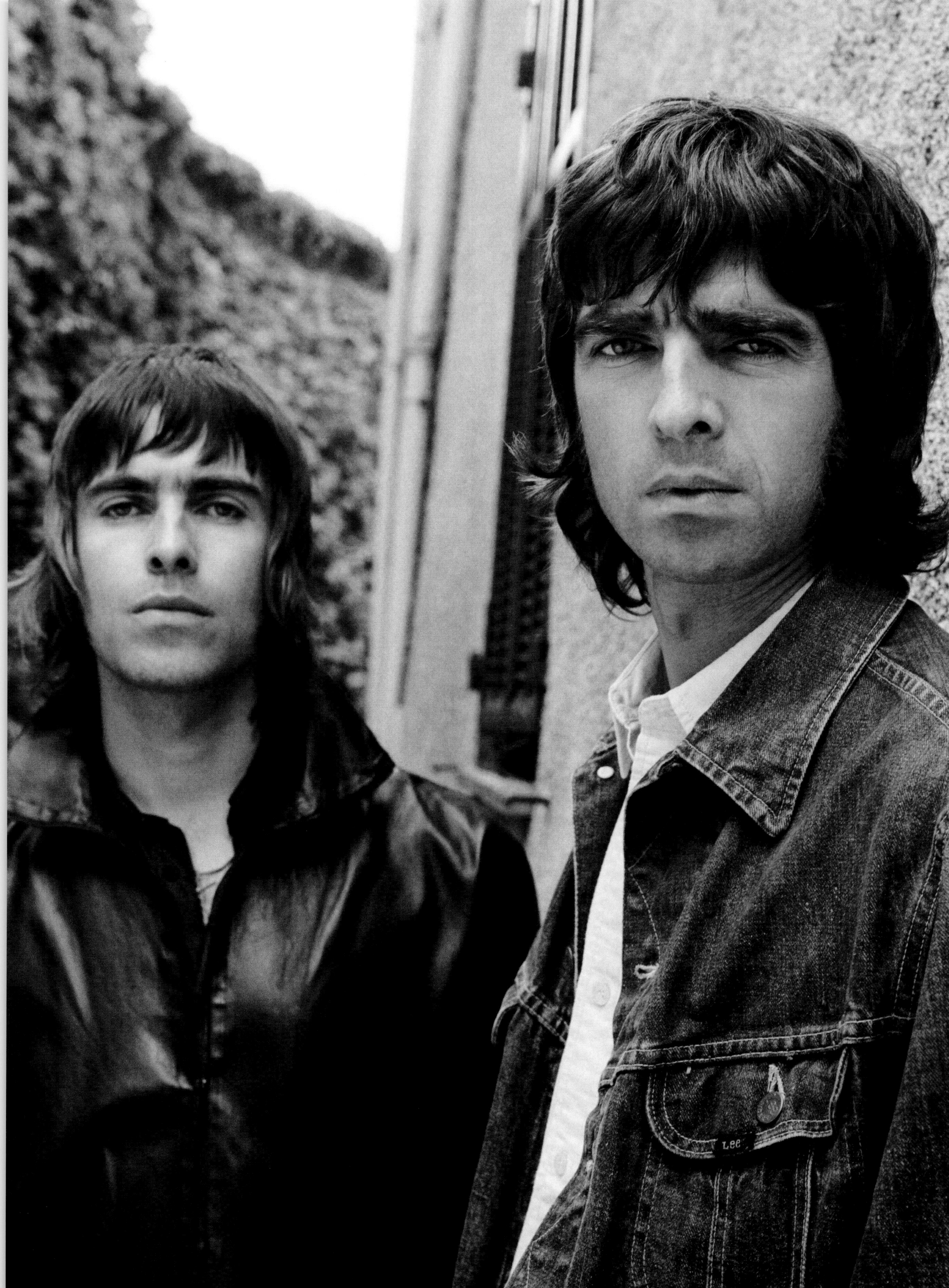
Lee

STANDING ON THE SHOULDER OF GIANTS

RELEASED	28 FEBRUARY 2000
RECORDED	APRIL–AUGUST 1999
STUDIOS	OLYMPIC STUDIOS (LONDON) SUPERNOVA HEIGHTS (LONDON) WHEELER END (BUCKINGHAMSHIRE) CHÂTEAU DE LA COLLE NOIRE (NEAR CANNES)
LENGTH	47:53
LABEL	BIG BROTHER RECORDINGS
PRODUCERS	MARK 'SPIKE' STENT NOEL GALLAGHER
ARTWORK	

1999	CHÂTEAU DE LA COLLE NOIRE / NEAR CANNES, FRANCE THE WORX / LONDON, UK
2000	REHEARSALS, BRAY STUDIOS / WINDSOR, UK WEMBLEY STADIUM / LONDON, UK #3 CHEMISTRY AND CHAOS / LAURA BARTON
2001	SHEPHERD'S BUSH EMPIRE / LONDON, UK MUSIC GROUND / LEEDS, UK MANCHESTER APOLLO / MANCHESTER, UK OLYMPIC STUDIOS / LONDON, UK
2002	FINSBURY PARK / LONDON, UK

THIS IS AT CHRISTIAN DIOR'S CHÂTEAU IN THE SOUTH OF FRANCE WHERE WE WENT TO RECORD *STANDING ON THE SHOULDER OF GIANTS*. IT WAS AN AMAZING GAFF. WE WERE THERE FOR LIKE FOUR MONTHS IN THE SUMMER, FUCKING HELL. ALL THE MONEY THAT WE'D MADE FROM *STORY MORNING GLORY*, WE FUCKING BLEW IT ON THAT RECORD.

→

20–22 MAY 1999
CHÂTEAU DE LA COLLE NOIRE
NEAR CANNES, FRANCE

The band were recording *Standing on the Shoulder of Giants* with Mark 'Spike' Stent at Christian Dior's mansion, La Colle Noir, near Cannes. When I arrived at the airport to do a shoot, I was told that Bonehead had just left the band! That was shocking, but as I was there with an assistant I decided to keep shooting, as I had from the start. I mainly concentrated on Noel and Liam, although I did shoot the four of them too, which felt strange. A few weeks later Guigs also left the band permanently, and the whole DNA changed. But for those few days, everybody was looking gorgeous. They had all been out in the sun and were eating well. They were very relaxed, despite the crisis that had happened, and I got some fantastic material. A little aside – told to *Dior* magazine later – apparently, Noel and Meg's daughter, Anaïs, was conceived there.

→

20–22 MAY 1999
CHÂTEAU DE LA COLLE NOIRE
NEAR CANNES, FRANCE

I was greatly influenced by David Hockney's photographic 'joiner' images of the early eighties. To me they reflect how we actually see the world, not in frozen moments but rather in a series of alternate wide-angle and detailed glances, which our brains assemble. This joiner shows Noel, Alan White, Guigs and Liam in the grand dining room of Christian Dior's house where they were recording.

oasis
ORANGE
WORKING

20–22 MAY 1999
CHÂTEAU DE LA COLLE NOIRE
NEAR CANNES, FRANCE

16 NOVEMBER 1999
THE WORX
LONDON, UK

A few months after our time in France, followed by recording sessions at Olympic Studios and Wheeler End, Noel called me to say Oasis now had two new members to replace Bonehead and Guigs. They were Andy Bell and Colin 'Gem' Archer (p. 216, right). As gigs were coming up, new pictures were needed urgently, and we decided to shoot simply on a white background to announce the new line-up to the world.

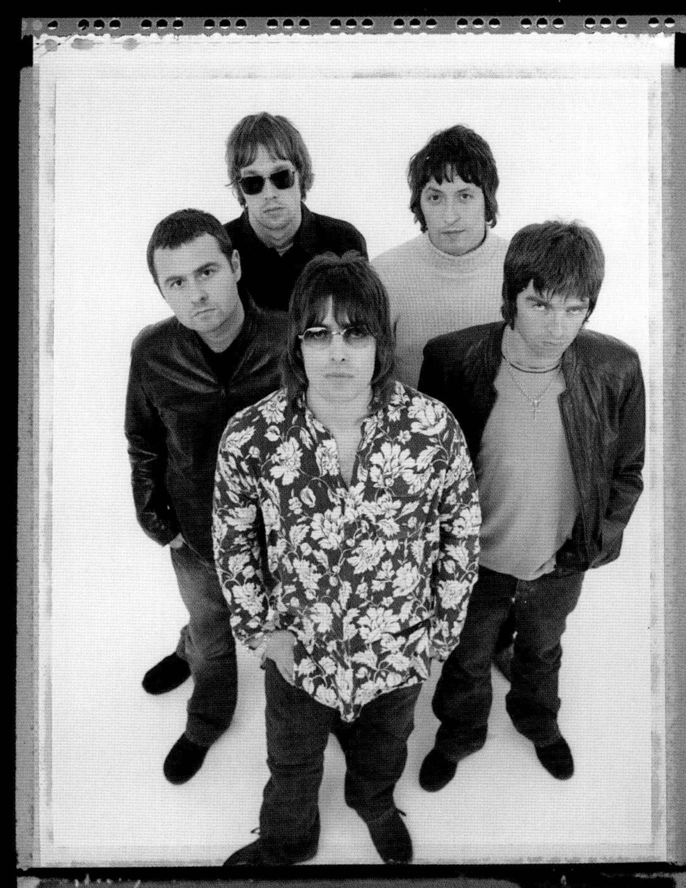

21 FEBRUARY 2000
REHEARSALS, BRAY STUDIOS
WINDSOR, UK

21 JULY 2000
WEMBLEY STADIUM
LONDON, UK

KODAK 160VC
KODAK 5042 EPJ
KODAK 400VC
KODAK 5063 TX
FUJI RHP

By 1998, that 'euphoric night out that started in '94', as Noel put it to the *Guardian* in 2008, was over. 'I need a proper fuckin' life,' he decided, looking around his home one day and realizing the rooms were filled with inebriated hangers-on. He sold his Belsize Park home, Supernova Heights, and moved to the country, hoping for a quieter, more sober existence. The party followed.

Creatively, Noel was at an impasse. Although *Be Here Now* had met with critical acclaim, it was not quite the commercial juggernaut it was expected to be. After their initial rapture, the critics, too, wondered if the album might be a little overblown. Chief among its detractors was Noel himself, who attributed its lack of lustre to too much pressure and an absence of effort. Out on the road, the thought occurred to him, 'It doesn't fucking stand up.'

Apathy is not an unusual condition for songwriters. The voracity that had propelled *Definitely Maybe* and *(What's the Story) Morning Glory?* had waned as the band grew familiar with success and other demands took over – its members exploring various combinations of fatherhood, marriage and divorce in the years that followed. Now, as the band considered their fourth album, Noel was faced with a conundrum: the uneasy relationship between comfort and creativity; the sense of having much to prove.

In the spring of 1999, the band rented Château de la Colle Noire, with its views out over the plains of Montauroux, its interiors designed by one-time owner Christian Dior, its scent of cypress and almond and rose. They took with them a collection of songs written by Noel over the summer and autumn of 1998, and demoed at the Wheeler End studio in Buckinghamshire in the company of long-serving collaborators Mark Coyle and Paul Stacey. With them in France was Mark 'Spike' Stent, the producer known for his work with U2, Madonna and the Spice Girls. Stent had been chosen to replace Owen Morris, who had steered the band's previous two records, in the hope of finding new vitality.

After a gruelling few months spent giving up drugs, Noel had adopted a policy he called 'Just Say No For the Foreseeable Future'. Liam, whose drinking had a tendency to unleash a heady chaos, had joined his older brother in agreeing to record the new album sober. Bonehead, however, was steadfast in his decision to keep boozing. Tensions ensued. Arguments erupted. After one particularly combustible showdown with Noel, the rhythm guitarist headed back to England.

That August, when Bonehead announced that he was officially leaving Oasis, he spoke of the desire to spend more time with his family. When bassist Guigs quit, by fax, a couple of weeks later, his reasons were much the same. 'It would have been better face to face,' Noel told a press conference in the back room of The Water Rats in London. 'He's been a mate for fifteen years. Yeah, we're shocked.'

With a new album due and the band set to begin a world tour, the timing of their bandmates' departure was challenging. 'We've been left holding the shit sandwich,' Noel told the assembled media. Announcing the hunt for their replacements, Liam stipulated that they would be required to have a good haircut and good shoes, and on no account could they support Manchester United.

To add to the shambles, when Noel had returned from the sessions in France he found himself disappointed with the recordings set down in the château. Listening back to the tapes, he concluded that they sounded altogether 'too posh'.

He set about trying to fix it, revisiting the demos on which he had recorded nearly all of the instruments himself. He refashioned the rhythm guitar and bass parts, drew on a collection of old guitars, small amps and strange pedals, and sought inspiration from recent collaborations with the Chemical Brothers and Goldie.

The result was the sound of a band in transition, ranging from lead single 'Fuckin' in the Bushes', which contained no lyrics but samples from *Message to Love*, a documentary about the Isle of Wight Festival of 1970, to 'Gas Panic!', in which Noel tried to capture the feeling of cocaine withdrawal. Along the way, there was the electronica of 'Who Feels Love?', a pop at the royal family on 'Go Let It Out' and the Liam-penned 'Little James'. The album took as its title a (misquoted) line by Sir Isaac Newton, which Noel had read on a £2 coin and drunkenly scrawled on the side of a cigarette packet. It struck him as a fine way to describe Oasis's position in the musical hierarchy: little boys, still, at the feet of the greats. 'I see us as a great band of the nineties,' he said. 'Let's see if we can span two decades.'

Standing on the Shoulder of Giants was the band's first album not on Creation. The label's founder, Alan McGee, announced that he would be winding up the company, and so Oasis started their own, Big Brother Recordings, backed by Sony. In a trademark flourish, it was decided that the catalogue number for each recording would begin with RKID.

By the time of the album's release, on the last day of February 2000, Noel seemed pragmatic about its merits. He distanced himself from some of it – memorably describing 'Put Yer Money Where Yer Mouth Is' and 'I Can See a Liar' as the album's 'two shit tracks' and was markedly restrained in his summation of the band's importance.

9 MAY 2005
WESTWAY STUDIOS
LONDON, UK

'If we were gonna have a massive, massive impact on music, we would've done it last time and we missed our chance,' he said. 'If this was the last record I was ever going to make, I would be thinking "Oh dear." But the next one's half-finished already.'

It would be another two years before *Heathen Chemistry* was released. In early December 1999, Oasis set out on a 133-date world tour. Andy Bell of Ride and Gem Archer of Heavy Stereo had replaced Guigs and Bonehead, and the band seemed rejuvenated by their presence.

By May, things were once again in disarray. Following an argument with Liam, Noel left the tour, drafting in guitarist Matt Deighton as his understudy, and announcing that he would only rejoin for shows in the UK and Ireland. Central to the brothers' disagreement appeared to be Liam's decision to return to drinking in the face of Noel's continuing sobriety. Later that year, a live album, *Familiar to Millions*, captured the band's two shows at Wembley Stadium. Elements from another performance at Yokohama had to be knitted into the recordings to cover Liam's drunkenness.

It was the singer's persistent inebriation that also delayed the release of the band's fifth album. In late 2001, Noel publicly lambasted his brother, telling how they had been waiting three-and-a-half months for Liam to complete his vocal parts. As it stood, he said, it was 'a fantastic album of instrumentals'.

In later years, Liam would rank *Heathen Chemistry* as his least favourite Oasis album. Noel, meanwhile, felt the band had 'recaptured something special' that had been lost on the previous two records. Reviewers were less convinced.

Still, today some of the band's most-loved songs can be found on *Heathen Chemistry*. 'Stop Crying Your Heart Out' marked a return to Noel's most affecting form of songwriting, in which lines that may seem prosaic on the page draw flame when sung aloud by his brother. It is a song of great yearning and quiet defeat, of solace and camaraderie. There are shades of 'Slide Away' and 'Wonderwall', of 'Half the World Away' and 'Don't Look Back in Anger'. In a World Cup summer, the song also seemed to capture much of the national mood, soundtracking England's exit in the quarter final.

Heathen Chemistry was a record, too, that seemed to offer a blueprint for the band's future work. Noel had relished the recording sessions – the regular hours, the lack of chaos, the experience of sharing writing duties with his younger brother and his bandmates. If Oasis were to continue, it seemed a fine way to steady the ship.

The follow-up, *Don't Believe the Truth*, took a while to come together. Drummer Alan White left the band, to be replaced by Zak Starkey. His departure was never fully explained, but it was rumoured to be due to musical differences. Early sessions with Death in Vegas offered few gems. Where they might once have ploughed on regardless, now the band members decided to take some time away, to recalibrate and reconvene afresh with a new producer, Dave Sardy. It proved a fruitful move. By the summer of 2004, they were sufficiently enthusiastic about the material to play two new tracks – 'The Meaning of Soul' and 'A Bell Will Ring' – at live shows in Poole and at Glastonbury festival.

Released in late May 2005, *Don't Believe the Truth* was greeted with a certain relief. For the first time in a while, Oasis seemed not so much galvanized as sturdy. The new songs held plenty of familiar touchstones – the Stranglers, the Velvet Underground, the Rolling Stones, the Kinks – but they appeared to have drawn on them out of genuine enthusiasm, rather than out of habit. 'We seem to have reacquired the spirit,' as Noel put it. The attendant tour was remarkable for its lack of incident, and for being the first time the band played New York's Madison Square Garden.

While band relations remained spirited and congenial, it seemed wise to continue. Recording sessions for the new album *Dig Out Your Soul* began six months after completing the final leg of the *Don't Believe the Truth* tour, the band setting up in Abbey Road Studios and turning once again to Sardy for production. Noel had already expressed a desire to make a 'colossal' album, complete with orchestras and choirs and the whole 'kitchen sink'. Later that year, he spoke of how, with little fresh material to write about, he had been revisiting the psychedelic trips of his youth, while Liam told of the record's heaviness and absence of acoustic tracks. Fans wondered what, precisely, to expect.

When it arrived, the band's sixth album was not as grand or as avant-garde as some might have predicted. It included samples from John Lennon's final interview and some krautrock dabbling, but the essential Oasis sound remained undimmed. The subsequent tour began in late August 2008, with new live drummer Chris Sharrock. It saw the band break the record for ticket sales in a single day – 500,000 in just seven hours – and encompassed three shows at Manchester's Heaton Park. On the first night, when generator failures twice led the band to leave the stage, Liam returned for the third time and announced to the 70,000-strong audience that the concert was now free. Some 20,000 of them claimed a refund.

After a period of stability, there was something fractious about the *Dig Out Your Soul* tour. In Toronto, a crowd member broke through security and knocked Noel to the ground. For a moment, the band faltered, dates were cancelled and postponed, and a strange shadow seemed to fall over the remainder of the tour. Later, the Chinese authorities would revoke the band's performing visas after learning that Noel had played at a Free Tibet performance, and in August 2009, a laryngitis diagnosis would force Liam to cancel a turn at V Festival in Essex.

Just five days after V, Oasis were due to play Rock en Seine festival in Paris. But, midway through Bloc Party's set at the festival, singer Kele Okereke announced the band would not be performing.

Backstage, Liam and Noel had sparred over the younger Gallagher's decision to advertise his clothing range in the Oasis tour programme. Soon, they were wrestling in the dressing room. Later, Noel would recall how Liam left the room – hurling a plum against the wall as he stormed out of the door. He did not expect his brother to return, and most certainly did not expect him to do so wielding his own guitar 'like an axe'. Noel left the venue and sat outside in a car.

Two hours later, he released a statement: 'It's with some sadness and great relief to tell you I quit Oasis tonight. People will write and say what they like, but I simply could not go on working with Liam a day longer.' Fifteen years after their explosive debut, the defiance and possibility and propulsion had finally come to rest.

Mic Stand

↑→

7–8 OCTOBER 2001
SHEPHERD'S BUSH EMPIRE
LONDON, UK

(FUCKIN' IN THE BUSHES)
GO LET IT OUT
COLUMBIA
MORNING GLORY
ACQUIESCE
SUPERSONIC
FADE AWAY
THE HINDU TIMES
HALF THE WORLD AWAY
ONE WAY ROAD
THE MASTERPLAN
GAS PANIC!
CIGS & ALCOHOL
LIVE FOREVER
HUNG IN A BAD PLACE
SLIDE AWAY
SHE'S ELECTRIC
CHAMPAGNE SUPERNOVA
ROCK N' ROLL STAR
DON'T LOOK BACK IN ANGER
I AM THE WALRUS
OASIS
10 Years of Noise
Sunday, 7th
Shepherds Bush
LOAD IN 8:00
OASIS
SOUND CHECK 4:00-
THE MUSIC
SOUND CHECK 5:30-
DOORS 7:00
THE MUSIC
ON STAGE 8:00-
OASIS
ON STAGE 9:00-

Gibson
Standard

10 OCTOBER 2001
MUSIC GROUND
LEEDS, UK

←↓

10 OCTOBER 2001
MANCHESTER APOLLO
MANCHESTER, UK

3–6 DECEMBER 2001
OLYMPIC STUDIOS
LONDON, UK

3–6 DECEMBER 2001
OLYMPIC STUDIOS
LONDON, UK

39

↑

3–6 DECEMBER 2001
OLYMPIC STUDIOS
LONDON, UK

The band were working with Johnny Marr on a version of 'It's All Too Much', a song by George Harrison. It was intended as a homage to George who had died in late November. A few lines of the song are visible in the bottom right corner of the joiner photo. I set up a tripod in the middle of the room and, over the course of the day, shot individual frames, from left to right, top to bottom, in the same way a scanner moves. As a result, the musicians were shot multiple times in different positions. I had the film developed and printed as 5 × 7-in. and 6 × 4-in. glossy prints. Between Christmas and New Year, I assembled the prints on the dining room table to make an artwork. It was like making a deeply satisfying jigsaw puzzle. I wonder what happened to that recording....

3–6 DECEMBER 2001
OLYMPIC STUDIOS
LONDON, UK

VOX
WEM

M.S LTD.

6 JULY 2002
FINSBURY PARK
LONDON, UK

←→

6 JULY 2002
FINSBURY PARK
LONDON, UK

HEATHEN

RELEASED	1 JULY 2002
RECORDED	2001–2002
STUDIOS	WHEELER END (BUCKINGHAMSHIRE) OLYMPIC STUDIOS (LONDON)
LENGTH	47:54 (76:36 WITH HIDDEN TRACK)
LABEL	BIG BROTHER RECORDINGS
PRODUCER	OASIS
ARTWORK	

2004 WHEELER END / BUCKINGHAMSHIRE, UK
GLASTONBURY FESTIVAL / SOMERSET, UK
HIGH WYCOMBE / BUCKINGHAMSHIRE, UK
STRONGROOM / LONDON, UK

CHEMISTRY

6 APRIL 2004
WHEELER END
BUCKINGHAMSHIRE, UK

↓

26 APRIL 2004
WHEELER END
BUCKINGHAMSHIRE, UK

25 JUNE 2004
GLASTONBURY FESTIVAL
SOMERSET, UK

AUGUST 2004
HIGH WYCOMBE
BUCKINGHAMSHIRE, UK

1 SEPTEMBER 2004
STRONGROOM
LONDON, UK

1 SEPTEMBER 2004
STRONGROOM
LONDON, UK

DON'T BELIEVE THE TRUTH

RELEASED	30 MAY 2005
RECORDED	JANUARY 2004–JANUARY 2005
STUDIOS	OLYMPIC STUDIOS (LONDON) STRANGEWAY STUDIOS (MANCHESTER) WHEELER END (BUCKINGHAMSHIRE) CAPITOL STUDIOS (LOS ANGELES) METROPOLIS STUDIOS (LONDON) THE VILLAGE (LOS ANGELES)
LENGTH	42:52
LABEL	BIG BROTHER RECORDINGS
PRODUCERS	DAVE SARDY NOEL GALLAGHER
ARTWORK	

2005	HEINEKEN MUSIC HALL / AMSTERDAM, NETHERLANDS
2007	ABBEY ROAD / LONDON, UK

↑→

2 NOVEMBER 2005
HEINEKEN MUSIC HALL
AMSTERDAM, NETHERLANDS

These shots were taken backstage at the Heineken Music Hall in Amsterdam midway through the band's 11-month *Don't Believe the Truth* tour. They show long-time friends Phil Smith, who often DJ'd for the band, and Jonathan 'Scully' Mowatt, who is wearing a polo shirt in the photos. The latter now directs Noel's videos and is a well-known character at Manchester City. Both Noel and Liam remain close with these early-days friends.

AUGUST–DECEMBER 2007
ABBEY ROAD
LONDON, UK

KORG

Steinway & Sons.
Patent.
New York & Hamburg.

DIG OUT YOUR SOUL

RELEASED	6 OCTOBER 2008
RECORDED	JULY 2007–MARCH 2008
STUDIO	ABBEY ROAD (LONDON) HILLSIDE MANOR (LOS ANGELES) THE VILLAGE (LOS ANGELES)
LENGTH	45:51
LABEL	BIG BROTHER RECORDINGS
PRODUCER	DAVE SARDY
ARTWORK	

2008	BLACK ISLAND STUDIOS / LONDON, UK
2009	HEATON PARK / MANCHESTER, UK WEMBLEY STADIUM / LONDON, UK BRIDLINGTON SPA / YORKSHIRE, UK

14 AUGUST 2008
BLACK ISLAND STUDIOS
LONDON, UK

→→

14 AUGUST 2008
BLACK ISLAND STUDIOS
LONDON, UK

OF ALL THE PLACES – YOUR HOMETOWN. THE GENERATOR BROKE. SO WE CAME OFF STAGE AND THEN THE BACK-UP GENERATOR BROKE AS WE WENT BACK OUT. WE WENT OUT A THIRD TIME AND THEY SAID, 'WHATEVER YOU DO, DON'T LEAVE THE STAGE' BECAUSE THERE WAS TENSION IN THE CROWD. SOMEBODY SAID, 'IF THE GENERATOR BREAKS DOWN AGAIN, THAT'S IT. WE WILL JUST HAVE TO OFFER EVERYBODY THEIR MONEY BACK, AND IT'LL BE LIKE A FREE GIG.' LIAM GOT THE WRONG END OF THE STICK AND SAID, 'THIS IS NOW A FREE GIG.'

→ / →→ / →→→

4 JULY 2009
HEATON PARK
MANCHESTER, UK

oasis
ALMOST THERE!
PRESS
PRESS
PRESS

CHEESEBURGERS • HOTDOGS • FRIES
COUNTRY GRILL
EVENT STAFF

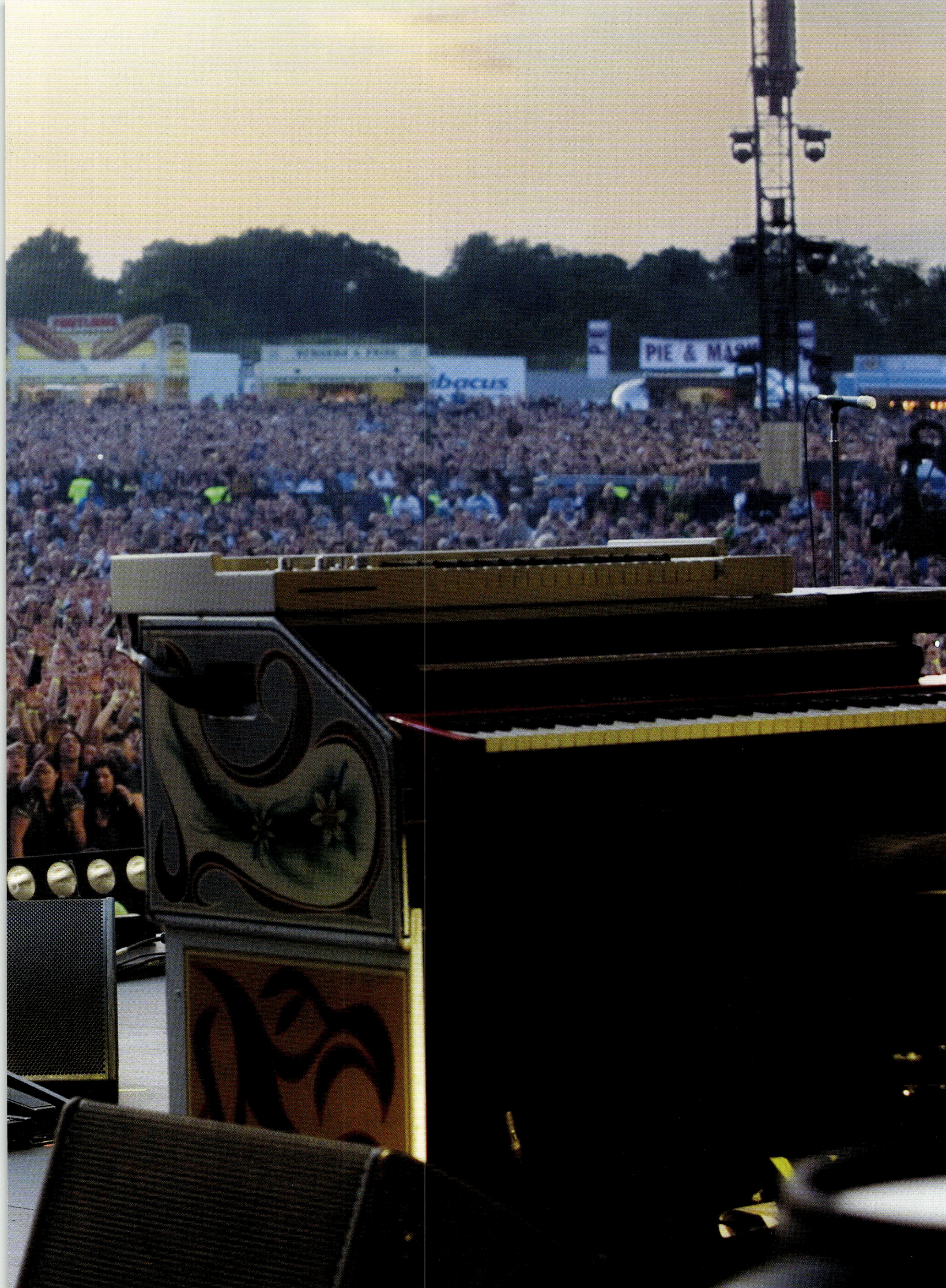

11–12 JULY 2009
WEMBLEY STADIUM
LONDON, UK

STAGE
oasis

SHOW & EVENT
SUPERVISOR
STAGE

↑ / →→ / →→→

20 AUGUST 2009
BRIDLINGTON SPA
YORKSHIRE, UK

On 20 August 2009, Oasis played their last 'own show' at Bridlington Spa in Yorkshire. It was particularly hot, and fans lucky enough to have a ticket made a day of it. Some took a dip in the sea; others milled about on the front, displaying their Pretty Green T-shirts, parkas and badged hats. The band could see them from the huge dressing-room windows that overlooked the sea wall and the beach. There was tension that day, backstage and on stage. During the show, Noel and Liam stood as far apart as possible. Nevertheless, it was a great gig. My lenses fogged up so badly that I retreated to the balcony to wipe them down and stayed there until the end. The band left immediately afterwards. Oasis played one more show in the UK, on 22 August at V Festival. Six days later, before going on stage in Paris on 28 August, the band suddenly imploded, leaving fans all over the world bereft.

MANCHESTER CITY F.C.

oasis

IN THE YEARS THAT FOLLOWED THAT DARK EVENING IN PARIS, FANS HAVE LOOKED FOR SIGNS OF RAPPROCHEMENT BETWEEN THE GALLAGHER BROTHERS. LIAM SPOKE OF THE DEJECTION THAT FILLED HIS POST-OASIS DAYS, OF HOW HIS WORLD 'CAVED IN'. TO FILL THE VOID, HE ENLISTED ARCHER, BELL AND SHARROCK TO FORM BEADY EYE, BEFORE EMBARKING ON A SOLO CAREER. NOEL, MEANWHILE, LAUNCHED HIGH FLYING BIRDS, ITS TOURING BAND ALSO FEATURING ARCHER AND SHARROCK.

THEY WERE MUSICIANS, STILL, BUT FOR MANY, THE SPIRIT OF OASIS LIVED ON MORE TANGIBLY IN THE INSULTS THE BROTHERS WOULD TRADE IN THE PRESS. THE PAIR MADE AN ARTFORM OF THE PUT-DOWN AND THE TAUNT. NOEL DISMISSED LIAM'S SOLO OUTPUT AS 'UNSOPHISTICATED MUSIC. FOR UNSOPHISTICATED PEOPLE. MADE BY AN UNSOPHISTICATED MAN.' LIAM SIMPLY ADDRESSED HIS ESTRANGED BROTHER AS 'TOFU BOY.' IT WAS A DUET OF SORTS; A REMINDER THAT THE ELECTRICITY BETWEEN THEM STILL FLICKERED.

FOR FIFTEEN YEARS, NO CONVERSATION WITH A GALLAGHER BROTHER WAS COMPLETE WITHOUT ADDRESSING THE LIKELIHOOD OF A THAWING IN FRATERNAL RELATIONS AND, WITH IT, AN OASIS REUNION. IN THE EARLY DAYS, THE IDEA WAS ROUNDLY REJECTED BY BOTH PARTIES, BUT MORE RECENTLY THEIR POSITIONS HAD SEEMED TO SOFTEN. IN THE EARLY PART OF LAST YEAR, LIAM SPOKE OF HOW HE WOULD LIKE TO BE BACK IN CONTACT WITH NOEL. 'HE'S MY BROTHER,' HE SAID. 'I LOVE HIM.'

WHEN THE OASIS REUNION WAS ANNOUNCED, IN LATE AUGUST 2024, IT FELT WELL-TIMED; MORE LOVE-IN THAN CASH-IN; THE RESULT OF A GRADUAL CLOSENING. IT SEEMED, TOO, TO MEET A BROADER NEED: NOT FOR COMEBACK TOURS OR BRITPOP REVIVALS, BUT SOME DEEPER QUALITY GROWN SCARCE – A RECIPROCITY, A SENSE OF CONNECTION, A DEVOTION FOUND THROUGH MUSIC.

ONCE, NOEL EXPLAINED HOW THE COLLECTIVISM HE HAD FIRST EXPERIENCED THROUGH THE ACID HOUSE ERA OF THE LATE EIGHTIES AND EARLY NINETIES HAD BEEN THE FORCE BEHIND OASIS. IT WASN'T ABOUT SWAGGERING EGOTISM, HE EXPLAINED. 'IT WAS ABOUT UNITY…IT WAS ABOUT "YOU AND ME".' THOSE WHO DISMISSED OASIS AS LAD ROCK, OR WHO HAD BEEN DISTRACTED BY THE GALLAGHERS' BICKERING, HAD LONG MISSED THE POINT. TO LOVE THIS BAND WAS TO EMBRACE A SPIRIT THAT WAS GENEROUS AND INCLUSIVE.

TO RETURN TO THAT LOVE, TO STAND IN A CROWD BEFORE THEM AGAIN, IS A POWERFUL THING. THE OASIS REUNION IS AN INVITATION OF SORTS – TO JOIN TOGETHER, TO FEEL THAT UNITY AGAIN, TO FIND THE SELVES WE ONCE WERE. 'PEOPLE NEVER FORGET', NOEL ONCE SAID, 'THE WAY YOU MADE THEM FEEL.'

LAURA BARTON

↑

27 MAY 2025
REUNION REHEARSAL
LONDON, UK

CAPTIONS

ALBUM PAGES

P. 12

22 JULY 1995
SLANE CASTLE
NEAR DUBLIN, IRELAND

P. 68

4 AUGUST 1996
BALLOCH CASTLE COUNTRY PARK
LOCH LOMAND, SCOTLAND

P. 144

FEBRUARY 1997
AIR STUDIOS
LONDON, UK

P. 208

20–22 MAY 1999
CHÂTEAU DE LA COLLE NOIRE
NEAR CANNES, FRANCE

P. 246

15–17 JUNE 2004
REHEARSALS, THE DEPOT
LONDON, UK

P. 260

AUGUST–DECEMBER 2007
ABBEY ROAD
LONDON, UK

P. 270

14 AUGUST 2008
BLACK ISLAND STUDIOS
LONDON, UK

PRELIMS & MONTAGE PAGES

P. 2

Montage of test strips of Oasis taken over fifteen years, assembled by photographer Andi Blake.

PP. 4–5

A selection of song notes discarded on the studio floor during rehearsal at the Depot on 28 September 1995.

P. 9

Noel rehearsing at the NEC, Birmingham, 28 July 1996.

P. 32
CLOCKWISE FROM TOP LEFT:
Bonehead, Guigs and Noel at the 'Live Forever' video shoot, Portland Place, London, 5 January 1995;
Overhead shot of the band at Portland Place, London, 5 January 1995;
Multiple frames of the band during the US tour, March 1996;
Noel at the Creation Christmas party, London, 22 December 1995;
The band on the streets of San Francisco, 31 January 1995;
Noel on stage at Maine Road, Manchester, 26 April 1996;
Dick Green, Liam, Johnny Hopkins, Noel, Meg Mathews and Alan McGee at the Creation Christmas party, London, 22 December 1995;
Multiple frames of the Ignition office with Knebworth poster in background and featuring Alec McKinlay and Christine Biller, London, August 1996;
Liam during the 'Wonderwall' video shoot, London, 29 September 1995;
Transparencies of Noel and Guigs at the Corn Exchange, Cambridge, 4 December 1994.

P. 160
CLOCKWISE FROM TOP LEFT:
Alan McGee and Dick Green, backstage at Maine Road, Manchester, 26 April 1996;
Paolo Hewitt, Daniela Soave, Bonehead and Alan McGee backstage at the Corn Exchange, Cambridge, 4 December 1994;
The band in the empty stands before the gig at Maine Road, Manchester, 26 April 1996;
The band kick a football into the audience at Knebworth, Hertfordshire, 10 August 1996;
Johnny Hopkins, Creation PR, Cambridge, 4 December 1994;
Liam takes a moment to reflect in San Francisco, 31 January 1995;
Two frames showing Noel with Paul Mathur at a book signing for *Take Me There: Oasis, the Story*, 26 November 1996;
Bonehead on stage at Earls Court, London, 27 September 1997;
Alan White on stage at Wembley Arena, London, 18 December 1997;
Liam accosts a cyclist in Paris, 23 November 1995;
Multiple frames of Maine Road, Manchester, 27 April 1996.

P. 222
CLOCKWISE FROM TOP LEFT:
Two frames of Liam recording at Olympic Studios, London, 5 December 2001;
Liam and Noel before the gig at Wembley Stadium, London, 21 July 2000;
Noel and Liam with producer Dave Sardy in Studio 2, Abbey Road Studios, London, 9 August 2007;
Multiple frames of Noel at Wheeler End Studio, Buckinghamshire, 23 April 2004;
Multiple frames of Johnny Marr at Music Ground guitar shop, Leeds, 10 October 2001;
Noel and Liam watch TV with Alan White backstage at Wembley Stadium, 21 July 2000;
Two frames of Alan White at Olympic Studios, London, 5 December 2001;
The band rehearse at Westway Studios, London, 9 May 2005;
Noel and Johnny Marr at Music Ground guitar shop, Leeds, 10 October 2001;
Two frames of Noel and Liam at Olympic Studios, London, 27 July 1999.

SOURCES OF ILLUSTRATIONS

Every effort has been made to locate and credit copyright holders of the material reproduced in this book. The author and publisher apologize for any omissions or errors, which can be corrected in future editions.

All photography by Jill Furmanovsky unless otherwise stated below.

P. 2
Test strips by Jill Furmanovsky. Montage by Andi Blake.

P. 11
Photograph by Paul Mathur.

P. 13
Definitely Maybe, Oasis, Creation Records Ltd. Photograph: Michael Spencer Jones. Sleeve concept, design and art direction: Brian Cannon for Microdot.

P. 69
(What's The Story) Morning Glory?, Oasis, Creation Records Ltd. Photograph: Michael Spencer Jones. Model: Sean Rowley. Sleeve design and art direction: Brian Cannon for Microdot, assisted by Matthew Sankey.

P. 145
Be Here Now, Oasis, Creation Records Ltd. Photograph: Michael Spencer Jones. Sleeve design and art direction: Brian Cannon for Microdot, assisted by Matthew Sankey and Martin Catherall.

P. 209
Standing on the Shoulder of Giants, Oasis, Big Brother Recordings Ltd. Photograph: Andrew MacPherson. Art direction: Simon Halfon and Noel Gallagher.

P. 247
Heathen Chemistry, Oasis, Big Brother Recordings Ltd. Photograph: Andrew MacPherson. Sleeve design: Noel Gallagher and Simon Halfon.

P. 261
Don't Believe the Truth, Oasis, Big Brother Recordings Ltd. Photograph: Lawrence Watson. Artwork concept and design: Noel Gallagher. Layout: Simon Halfon. Painting (of garages): Luke Dane.

P. 271
Dig Out Your Soul, Oasis, Big Brother Recordings Ltd. Artwork: Julian House for Intro.

PP. 296–7
Photograph by Jill Furmanovsky and Mel Yates.

P. 299
Photograph by Yvonne Catterson.

AUTHOR AND CONTRIBUTOR BIOS

↓

OCTOBER 2023
NOEL AND JILL IN JILL'S STUDIO
LONDON, UK

Jill Furmanovsky has photographed legendary rock musicians for more than 50 years, including Pink Floyd, Bob Dylan, Blondie, The Clash, The Police, The Ramones, The Pretenders, Joy Division, Leonard Cohen, Amy Winehouse and Oasis. In 2024 she received a Lifetime Achievement award from *Amateur Photography* magazine; the Legend of the Year award from So.Co Image of Music Awards; and the prestigious Abbey Road ICON award at which ceremony Noel described Jill as 'one of my best friends'.

Noel Gallagher is the primary songwriter, lead guitarist and co-lead vocalist of Oasis, the band that defined the era of Cool Britannia. In August 1994 Oasis's first album, *Definitely Maybe*, entered the UK charts at No.1 and received widespread critical and commercial success, as did their next two albums, *(What's the Story) Morning Glory?* (1995) and *Be Here Now* (1997). The band split in 2009 but have reformed for a worldwide tour in 2025.

Simon Spence is the *Sunday Times* bestselling author of *The Stone Roses: War and Peace*. His most recent book, *Feeing Supersonic: From Madchester to Britpop*, is available from backstagebooks.com. He is a former music journalist for *NME, The Face, i-D, Dazed* and many others.

Johnny Hopkins was Head of Press and Oasis's publicist at Creation Records during the nineties. Since 2000, at Triad Publicity, Johnny has represented clients including Sinead O'Connor, Lee 'Scratch' Perry, Graham Coxon, Kasabian, the Jesus and Mary Chain, Mark Stewart and Adrian Sherwood, as well as photographers Dennis Morris and Gered Mankowitz. He has written on the Velvet Underground, Elvis Presley, Britpop and the music industry.

Laura Barton has been a feature writer and music columnist for the *Guardian* for more than ten years. She also writes for the *Observer*, the *New York Times*, *1843* magazine, the *Telegraph*, the *Financial Times* and *Q* magazine, and is a regular contributor to Radio 4 and Radio 3. She speaks regularly at festivals and universities and since 2018 has curated the literary stage at Green Man festival. She is the author of two novels: *Twenty-One Locks*, published in 2011, and *Sad Songs*, which will be published in 2026.

BAND MEMBERS

NOEL GALLAGHER
Lead guitar and vocals (1991–2009, 2024–) / **Rhythm guitar** (1991, 1999–2009, 2024–) / **Keyboards** (1995–2009) / **Bass** (1993–1994, 1995, 1999)

LIAM GALLAGHER
Vocals, tambourine (1991–2009, 2024–) / **Acoustic guitar** (2001–2002, 2007–2008)

PAUL 'BONEHEAD' ARTHURS
Rhythm guitar (1991–1999, 2025–) / **Lead guitar** (1991) / **Keyboards** (1994–1997) / **Bass** (1995)

PAUL 'GUIGS' MCGUIGAN
Bass (1991–1995, 1995–1999)

TONY MCCARROLL
Drums (1991–1995)

ALAN 'WHITEY' WHITE
Drums, percussion (1995–2004)

GEM ARCHER
Rhythm and lead guitar (1999–2009, 2025–) / **Backing vocals** (2002–2003) / **Keyboards** (2002–2005) / **Harmonica** (2005–2009)

ANDY BELL
Bass (1999–2009, 2025–) / **Rhythm guitar** (2003–2009) / **Keyboards** (2007–2009)

SCOTT MCLEOD
Bass (1995)

MIKE ROWE
Keyboards (1997–2000, 2001)

MATT DEIGHTON
Rhythm guitar (2000)

ZEB JAMESON
Keyboards (2000–2001)

STEVE WHITE
Drums, percussion (2001)

JAY DARLINGTON
Keyboards (2002–2009)

ZAK STARKEY
Drums, percussion (2004–2008)

CHRIS SHARROCK
Drums, percussion (2008–2009)

JOEY WARONKER
Drums, percussion (2025–)

ACKNOWLEDGMENTS

I WOULD LIKE TO THANK THE FOLLOWING:

Noel Gallagher for his vision, practical support and friendship throughout the journey. Liam Gallagher for the rollercoaster ride and his underlying sweetness. Paul 'Bonehead' Arthurs, Paul 'Guigs' McGuigan, Tony McCarroll, Alan 'Whitey' White, Gem Archer, Andy Bell, Zak Starkey, Mike Rowe, Chris Sharrock and Jay Darlington. Peggy Gallagher for her kindness.

Maggie Mouzakitis, Jason Rhodes and the Oasis road crew past and present – I always felt like one of the team. Marcus Russell, Alec McKinlay, Kat Killingley, Clare Byrne and Sarah Mansfield at Ignition. Debbie Gwyther at Fear PR. Sam and Roy Eldridge at UROK Management. Alan McGee, Dick Green and Johnny Hopkins at Creation Records. Brian Cannon at Microdot.

Daniela Soave for introducing me to the band.

Melissa Green for highly skilled production and retouching. Many thanks!

Lianne Snelson and Clare Guise at rockarchive.com. Vicki McIvor from Take 3 Management. Gail Buckland.

Tristan de Lancey, Agatha Smith, Jane Laing, Sadie Butler and Florence Allard at Thames & Hudson.

Yvonne Catterson, Tracey Kraft, Stuart Nicholls, Jane Ripley, Mel Yates, Andi Blake and Stuart Culley. Film-makers: Robin Guise and LipSync; Yvonne and Matt McConnaghy.

Simon Spence, Johnny Hopkins and Laura Barton for their excellent essays.

Mark Robertson and Abbey Road Studios.

Aubrey 'Po' Powell, Anaïs Gallagher, Neville Brody, Johnny and Sonny Marr, and Mary McGuigan.

Virgilio Ponce (VP x), Leah Berglas McKinson, India Cowan, Cameron and Ty McKinson. Michele Esterman and The Mabels, Ruth Davis, Nick Segal, Sarah Lee and Ian Hessenberg.

↑

NOVEMBER 1997
PEGGY GALLAGHER
MANCHESTER, UK

←

SEPTEMBER 1997
'WAS THERE THEN' EXHIBITION
ROUNDHOUSE
LONDON, UK

In November 1997 I went to Peggy Gallagher's house in Burnage, south Manchester, where she still lives, to bring her some prints. At the time I was installing my 'Was There Then' exhibition at the legendary Hacienda Club. I'd met Peggy several times during the early years, mainly at gigs. She is one of the most down-to-earth people you could ever meet. I always enjoyed talking to her.

Some of my pictures were on the walls in the house mixed with other family snaps. She allowed me to see 'Noel & Liam's' room. There was a huge wardrobe on the right containing a quantity of Liam's clothes – 'He keeps saying he'll collect them but he hasn't.' There were Beatles posters on the walls. It was a tiny room. 'It didn't used to have a wardrobe,' she explained. 'That was where Liam's bed was; Noel was in that corner. They kept away from each other.'

She said she never imagined a time when she wouldn't have to work – thought she'd be doing it in her seventies. She used to have four jobs – cleaning lady, dinner lady, more cleaning and then working in an old people's home at night.

In the back garden Liam's abandoned scooter leant against a wall behind the washing line. Peggy agreed to sit on it for the one frame I had left in my Hasselblad from an earlier shoot.

INDEX

PAGE NUMBERS FOR ILLUSTRATIONS ARE SHOWN IN *ITALICS*.

A

B

C

D

E

F

G

H

I

K

L

M

N

O

P

R

S

V

W

This book is dedicated to my grandchildren India and Cameron and especially to my daughter Leah, who sometimes accompanied me to Oasis rehearsals and gigs.

↓
28 SEPTEMBER 1995
LEAH VISITS OASIS REHEARSAL
THE DEPOT, LONDON, UK

First published in the United Kingdom in 2025 by
Thames & Hudson Ltd, 6–24 Britannia Street, London WC1X 9JD

First published in the United States of America in 2025 by
Thames & Hudson Inc., 500 Fifth Avenue, New York, New York 10110

For other image copyright information, see page 298

EU Authorized Representative: Interart S.A.R.L.
19 rue Charles Auray, 93500 Pantin, Paris, France
productsafety@thameshudson.co.uk
interart.fr

A CIP catalogue record for this book is available from the British Library

Library of Congress Control Number 2025940085

ISBN 978-0-500-03064-6
01

Printed and bound in Italy by Printer Trento Spa

MIX
Paper | Supporting responsible forestry
FSC® C015829